Leonardo da Vinci's Mental Models:
Secrets of the World's Most Famous Polymath

By Peter Hollins,

Author and Researcher at petehollins.com

Table of Contents

INTRODUCTION — 5

CHAPTER 1: FROM APPRENTICE TO MASTER — 13

- FIND YOUR MENTOR — 13
- THE WORLD IS YOUR CLASSROOM — 26
- BECOME A RENAISSANCE READER — 37

CHAPTER 2: THE MIND OF THE POLYMATH — 49

- THE HEART OF ALL LEARNING — 49
- THE ELASTIC MIND — 60
- SENSAZIONE — 70

CHAPTER 3: A MAP OF THE INTELLECT — 82

- BE A T-SHAPED HUMAN — 82
- CONNECTING THE UNCONNECTED — 95

CHAPTER 4: GET ORGANIZED — 108

- DA VINCIAN NOTE-TAKING — 108
- A TO-DO LIST IS ALSO A TO-LEARN LIST — 117

CHAPTER 5: STRIKING A BALANCE — 132

DOING AND NOT DOING — 132
ART AND SCIENCE — 145
MIRROR WRITING — 156

CONCLUSION — 166

SUMMARY GUIDE — 173

Introduction

"The painter has the universe in his mind and hands."

Leonardo da Vinci

Leonardo da Vinci is universally recognized as a genius painter, polymath, and the world's first and truest Renaissance man. But who was he really?

Beyond the abundant myths and conjecture about his life, da Vinci was a man who was defined by nothing if not his insatiable curiosity. He was not just a painter but an inventor, scientist, artisan, draughtsman, philosopher, botanist, sculptor, musician, and nature-lover. In fact, so diverse were his talents and interests that part of his appeal must lie in the fact that we sense in da Vinci something that transcends superficial categories and speaks to something more subtle and profound.

In this book, we'll be exploring the mind of arguably one of the greatest thinkers and creators of all time. His works are well known, and his biography has been told and retold countless times. Here, however, we will look not at what he thought, but how he thought . . . and perhaps glean some small insight to *why*. Da Vinci's life course has proved so fascinating that it's held our continued interest for more than five hundred years, with modern scholars returning to his work again and again to find fresh insight into our modern-day problems.

Whether you are a scientist, an artist, a little of both, or neither, you will hopefully find something in these pages to inspire you. By carefully studying the attitude and life philosophy of a man who was obsessed with learning, we can imbue our own lives with a little of that same passion and fire. Da Vinci demonstrated thinking that was broad as well as deep, flexible, and inquisitive, three dimensional and multisensory. He was self-directed and prolific, but also extremely meticulous in his organization. But the man was also an enigma, and historians continue to puzzle over some of his less well-understood tendencies and methods.

In the chapters that follow, we'll take da Vinci for our model and try to recreate some of his characteristics in our own lives, whether that's the ability to think holistically, to blur boundaries, or to cultivate the humility to continually subject yourself to a higher authority: not wealth or fame, but the deeper mysteries of the universe itself.

First of all, a little more about the man who inspired this book. Born the twenty-fourth of April in 1452, in the small Tuscan town of Vinci, Florence, the young genius had fairly humble beginnings. He was the son of rich legal notary

Messer Piero Fruosino di Antonio da Vinci and a poor orphaned servant girl, Caterina di Meo Lippi.

He was christened "Leonardo di ser Piero da Vinci," and his full name meant "Leonardo, son of Messer Piero from Vinci." The title "ser" showed that his father was considered a gentleman. His parents were unmarried, and his conception possibly occurred while his father was engaged to someone else, so Leonardo's position in the family was somewhat contentious. He lived with his mother till he was five, and then with his father, who had by then married a sixteen-year-old girl named Albiera. Altogether his father produced twelve more children and married four times, leaving Leonardo and his seven brothers to fight over his father's estate after his death.

The illegitimacy of his birth meant that Leonardo was officially recognized as da Vinci's son but received little attention, which resulted in a very informal education. He learned the rudiments of reading, writing, and arithmetic, but much of his learning occurred through his own efforts of observation and exploring the new ideas emerging in the Florentine milieu. At the age of fourteen, his father's connections allowed Leonardo to secure an apprenticeship under master painter Andrea del Verrocchio, who himself had studied under the sculptor Donatello.

Leonardo worked hard and eventually became a paid employee, gradually embedding himself in the emerging Renaissance art scene that included Botticelli, Ghirlandaio, Michaelangelo (a later rival), Masaccio, and Perugino. Da Vinci helped his master paint *The Baptism of Christ*, and legend has it that when Verrocchio saw the beauty of the angel Leonardo had created, he never painted again.

At the time, the ultra-powerful and influential Medici family controlled much of the city, and in 1481, da Vinci was commissioned by Lorenzo de' Medici (known as "Lorenzo the Magnificent") to paint an altarpiece for the church of San Donato. This work was never actually completed, however—a theme we will explore in a later chapter! From that point on, da Vinci was employed by Ludovico Sforza, where he produced some of his most famous works, including the *Virgin of the Rocks* and *The Last Supper*. He also painted pieces for a wide variety of notable people, including King Louis XII of France.

Leonardo was just sixty-seven when he died, reportedly full of repentance and mourning. Astonishingly, he is reported to have said, "I have offended God and mankind because my work did not reach the quality it should have." In his will he requested that sixty beggars bearing candles follow his casket during the funeral rites, and he was buried at the Chapel of Saint-Hubert in France.

Da Vinci's pupil and heir Francesco Melzi inherited everything da Vinci owned, including his tools, artworks, money, and countless books and notebooks. Da Vinci was celebrated during his lifetime and celebrated afterward. Georgio Vasari, an art historian and author of *Lives of the Most Eminent Painters, Sculptors, and Architects*, said of da Vinci:

> "The loss of Leonardo was mourned out of measure by all who had known him, for there was none who had done such honor to painting. The splendor of his great beauty could calm the saddest soul, and his words could move the most obdurate mind. His great strength could restrain the most violent fury, and he could bend an iron knocker or a horseshoe as if it were lead. He was liberal to his friends, rich and poor, if they had talent and worth; and indeed as Florence had the greatest of gifts in his birth, so she suffered an infinite loss in his death."

How to Use this Book
Though it's obvious the kind and extent of talents the creator bestowed on da Vinci, what talents have been given to *you*?

What burning questions have been placed at the center of your being so that all your curiosity points forever toward that true north?

Whether you believe in God or not, what kind of life would you have to have lived in order for you to say on your deathbed, "I have pleased God and mankind because my work reached the quality it should have"?

Now, these may be lofty questions to begin with, especially if you've only picked up this book in an effort to improve your memory or learn a little self-discipline. Our patron of learning and Renaissance mentor, da Vinci, however, was a man of **excellence**. His first challenge to us is to become clear on our purpose and our higher mission, and to strive for a certain transcendence—even if we are only beginning with small things.

Perhaps you are an aspiring painter or an artist yourself, or perhaps you're an entrepreneur who is looking for a jolt of creative thinking and some inspiration for looking outside the box. Perhaps you are a student following a formal educational path, or maybe, like da Vinci himself, you have graduated from the "school of life" and are now interested in ways to become a more refined original thinker. Maybe you're a poet, a philosopher, a tinkerer, a content creator, an athlete, a business owner, a parent, or an inventor. Maybe you want to learn a new language, write a novel, or just live a more creative, authentic life outside of convention.

Whoever you are and however you answer the above three questions, there is something in these chapters to inspire and encourage you. All that's required (for this book and for life in general) is an open mind, a willingness to experiment, and the courage to challenge yourself to take responsibility for your own intellectual development. Oh, and lots and lots of notebooks!

Chapter 1: From Apprentice to Master

Find Your Mentor

> *"We are like dwarves perched on the shoulders of giants, and thus we are able to see more and farther than the latter. And this is not at all because of the acuteness of our sight or the stature of our body, but because we are carried aloft and elevated by the magnitude of the giants."*
>
> *Bernard of Chartres*

When you think of Leonardo da Vinci, how do you imagine him? Perhaps it's easy to envision da Vinci as he was at the end of his career, once he was already well-known and accomplished. Perhaps it's easy to imagine that the young Leonardo always somehow knew that he was destined for greatness, and simply advanced to this famed endpoint as though it were a matter of fate.

In reality, he started out pretty much like everyone starts. In other words, it even took da Vinci himself time to become da Vinci! Even though we today know him as a masterful painter and a million other things, the man himself began as an apprentice to the artists and great thinkers *he* admired and considered his most esteemed teachers. That's why we'll begin our book at the most appropriate place: the beginning, when da Vinci was merely an apprentice.

During the Renaissance period, it was customary to apprentice talented young individuals under a master who would guide and tutor their learning. When he was just fourteen years old, da Vinci became an apprentice to Andrea del Verrocchio, at the time a respected master artist. This was lucky for the boy, and securing such a prestigious opportunity was due mostly to his father's standing in the community.

The artist–apprentice relationship was a serious and highly codified contract; typically, it required extreme diligence and honesty from the apprentice, and involved mundane tasks like grinding paint pigments, priming paint panels, and preparing the studio. The master was deferred to in all things and trusted to tailor his teaching to his pupil's aptitude and temperament, advancing his study as and when he saw fit. As da Vinci honed his skills, he would have gradually taken on more complex responsibilities, learning at Verrocchio's feet and potentially assisting him with paintings.

Over the six years of his apprenticeship, da Vinci's skills grew, and he evolved into a paid collaborator for Verrocchio. During the

Renaissance, it was common for assistants to help with commissions, with specific stipulations in the contract designating the apprentice's and master's responsibilities. This was artistic and moral training, but it also was an inculcation into a highly rarified industry. Initially, the young apprentice would have received nothing but room and board for his tireless work, but eventually, by around 1473, da Vinci was likely paid to help Verrocchio create the background of paintings.

In 1472, da Vinci presented his masterpiece, the *Annunciation*, to the Florence painters' guild. The term "masterpiece" originated in the Middle Ages when apprentices had to submit exemplary work for approval by their guild. The concept reflects the early roots of the modern concept of a thesis submitted for a master's degree at a university. Successful submission demonstrated adequate mastery, leading to the apprentice's promotion to master status and authorization to train others. Da Vinci joined the guild in 1472, marking an official recognition of his mastery.

While da Vinci continued working with Verrocchio for another four years, he eventually embarked on his own artistic journey, and the rest, as they say, is history. Da Vinci certainly went on to create his own unique style and become a master in his own right. But he first began not by exploring his own expression, but by imitating the work of his much more accomplished teacher. It was very common, for example, for students and apprentices' work to be almost indistinguishable from their masters. While this may seem a little odd for modern sensibilities, it was taken as a given in da Vinci's time that one couldn't develop one's own unique talents and contribution unless one had *first* learned how to properly reproduce and emulate the works that had come before.

The first step in our journey to mastery, then, is not to explore our own goals, desires, and perspectives more deeply, but to seek out a mentor. Willingly submitting to the program set for us by a more accomplished and (hopefully) wiser teacher is not just about ensuring we put ourselves through the right curriculum. It's also about learning to cultivate the humble, curious, and diligent mindset required of real mastery— the kind of mastery that was prevalent during that period in history that most reliably produced geniuses.

Of course, today the educational landscape is not structured the way it was hundreds of years ago, and attitudes have changed considerably. That said, it is always possible to recreate that special master-student relationship and find mentoring that will genuinely help you thrive. First, it's worth understanding that there are three distinct modes or steps in a healthy apprenticeship:

Deep Observation (The Passive Mode)

In this phase, individuals entering a new environment or career are advised to observe and absorb the rules, procedures, and social dynamics. The emphasis is on understanding the explicit and implicit rules governing success in the given field. Picasso, a painter who also received something of a classical training, is known to have said, "Learn the rules like a pro so you can break them like an artist."

During this period, the apprentice is encouraged to mute their colors, avoid seeking attention, and focus on learning by careful observation. To the student who only desires quick and easy results, ostentation, and novelty, this part of learning may seem boring and unglamorous. You are, however, doing so much more than merely imitating your master. You are paying deep attention to the stated rules of your craft, the underlying work culture, and the power relationships within the industry you're working in. It's a way to pay respects to the traditions of your chosen field of inquiry, but also a time of hard work and investment—back then, breaking the rules was considered a privilege you had to earn!

Skills Acquisition (The Practice Mode)

Once the initial observation phase is completed, the apprentice moves to the active acquisition of skills. The apprenticeship system of the Middle

Ages involved hands-on learning through imitation and repetition, but it also rested heavily on the relationship between the young learner and the master. Lessons were not just about the mere mechanics of the craft, but about the broader social, historical, cultural, religious, and metaphysical context of that art, and the many duties that came with it. In other words, one was not merely developing as a superficial artisan, but as a whole person with a comprehensive worldview and set of moral imperatives that accompanied their art.

Unlike many modern and purely academic institutions, apprenticeship was a learning process that heavily emphasized tacit knowledge, i.e., a feeling for the skill that is hard to express in words but only demonstrated through action.

Experimentation (The Active Mode)

This last phase involves transitioning to an even more active mode of experimentation and applying acquired skills. The apprentice is encouraged to take on more responsibility, initiate projects, and expose themselves to criticisms from peers or the public. They are beginning to stand on their own two feet, but gradually. The purpose is to gauge progress, identify knowledge gaps, and develop the ability to handle criticism constructively.

How long each of the above phases lasts will depend on you, your current skill level, the thing you are trying to master, your chosen mentor, your goals, and much more. A good mentor, however, will be able to pay close attention to your progress and regulate your advance so that you are always progressing in a diligent but appropriately challenging way.

Questions to Ask

The right mentor for you may not be a wizened old person with a beard and a serious hat. In fact, the best tutors and mentors may take all sorts of unexpected forms. Whether they are institutional mentors within academic or professional settings, or elective mentors found in all sorts of other interesting places, these guiding figures can contribute significantly to your personal and intellectual development—if you choose them wisely, that is.

To find mentors, explore various avenues that cater to your preferences and interests. Start by exploring online mentorship networks like "Find a Mentor," which connects professionals seeking guidance with experienced mentors. Attend professional networking events, where business leaders often seek new contacts and partnerships.

Join fitness classes or groups or engage in volunteer events through platforms like Volunteer Match, which can connect you with like-minded professionals, especially those who have retired and are looking to give back. Industry-specific meetups, conferences, and tradeshows are excellent for finding mentors tailored to your field.

Another alternative is to leverage social media platforms, such as Twitter and LinkedIn, to identify potential mentors based on keyword searches and engagement levels. Lastly, don't underestimate the possibility of meeting mentors in any public location, from public transportation to restaurants and bars. Word of mouth can be almost magical in its ability to connect you to the right people. Put out the word and seek recommendations. As the Sufi mystics like to say, "When the student is ready, the teacher appears."

Once you've found a potential mentor, ask yourself the following questions:

Do they truly command their own subject?

It goes without saying, but a mentor should genuinely possess superior knowledge in the subject compared to the mentee. Evaluation of the mentor's expertise involves assessing academic or artistic contributions, publications, and ongoing work. But the mentor's competence, rather than fame, should guide the selection process. This means that, depending on the subject, their credentials and education may not matter as much as their plainly evidenced skill. Be clear on your own goals and priorities, and identify a person who has demonstrated the competence you wish to develop in yourself.

Too many people get drawn into coaches and gurus whose only skill is arguably self-marketing. When the noise and bluster is removed, there may be very little in the way of genuine skill to recommend such a person. If you are an absolute beginner, it may be okay to select someone who is merely more skilled than yourself, but if possible, look for someone who truly excels in the area, rather than someone who is merely adequate.

Can they get the most out of their students?

A good mentor maximizes the potential of students and collaborators by understanding their intellectual and character traits. Remember that possessing a skill and knowing how to teach are two different things! Genuine mentoring involves pushing individuals to set and achieve ambitious goals, rather than just providing comfort and validation. The mentor–student relationship should focus on leaving the mentee with new insights after each interaction. You may be tempted to go with someone "nice" or who you get on well with, but focus instead on that person who will push you when you need to be pushed.

Are they able to respond well to competition from their students?

This is something few of us consider. While collaboration is essential, competition exists in mentor–mentee relationships. Healthy competition between generations is beneficial, but destructive competition, especially using social power, is cautioned against. External recognition can establish the mentee as an equal, not just a subordinate. How might your chosen mentor react to that? Do they have the maturity, wisdom, and grace to fully encourage your learning, wherever it may go?

Unfortunately, some teachers are a little too fond of the elevated position they have above their pupils and wish to maintain it forever; a teacher who genuinely wants their student to reach their full potential, without feeling threatened, is worth their weight in gold.

Are they open to approaches and attitudes other than their own?

Mentors should pass on accumulated knowledge but encourage diverse approaches, styles, and methodologies. Even a highly respected and esteemed teacher only possesses their single perspective and should actively encourage their student to learn widely, rather than subscribing to their own methods exclusively. The mentor's cultural background should be embraced, but mentees should also explore new frontiers of knowledge and avoid hindering progress. As you can see, a good mentor should possess both technical and relational abilities—they need to be able to manage and contain your learning in a way that prioritizes your unique growth, without their own limitations and blind spots jeopardizing the process.

Have any of their students become more accomplished professionals than them?

This last question sets up quite a high bar, but it's possibly the most important on this list. Be curious about where ex-students of your master have ended up. A successful mentor should produce alumni who surpass them (at least some of the time), indicating the effectiveness of the mentor–student relationship.

"Poor is the pupil who does not surpass his master," said da Vinci, and indeed he did surpass his first master, Andrea del Verrocchio. Entering the great artist's studio as a mere errand boy in 1466, he exceeded him less than ten years later. Says biographer Vasari in his book *Lives of the Most Eminent Painters, Sculptors, and Architects*:

> "He was placed, then, as has been said, in his boyhood, at the instance of Ser Piero,

to learn art with Andrea del Verrocchio, who was making a panel-picture of S. John baptizing Christ, when Leonardo painted an angel who was holding some garments; and although he was but a lad, Leonardo executed it in such a manner that his angel was much better than the figures of Andrea; which was the reason that Andrea would never again touch color, in disdain that a child should know more than he."

Even to the untrained eye, the differences in the figure of Christ and the angel are apparent: Verrocchio's rendering of the hair is flat and lifeless compared to the almost supernatural way that the young da Vinci infused the angel's hair with glowing light. Biographer Walter Isaacson later added, "Afterward Verrocchio never completed any new painting on his own. More to the point, a comparison between the parts of *The Baptism of Christ* that Leonardo painted with those done by Verrocchio shows why the older artist would have been ready to defer."

Watch out for teachers who can only produce students who are copies of themselves and who never quite advance beyond their own level. Beware, also, of mentors who break ties with students the moment they surpass them. Ideally, a mentor's previous students should all become part of their extended network and continue to maintain a collaborative spirit long after training is over. It's a red flag if a tutor only trains those capable of becoming tutors themselves—an accomplished student should be able to achieve more than nominal success in the very same arena as his teacher!

The World Is Your Classroom

"Genius is not only a what or a who, it is a where. It is grounded in a place every single time."

Eric Weiner

A mentor is someone who can guide and shape your learning; by that definition, however, our environment itself can be considered a kind of mentor, in that it also influences the kind of people we can become and the sorts of things we can know. Here, "the environment" refers not just to the room you practice your craft in or the café you sometimes take a book to. It includes your entire socio-cultural milieu, your historical period, your social network, and your family. Rather than imagining that a genius is a rare and perfectly individual phenomenon springing up from nowhere, we can see it instead as a kind of flower that blooms on a much larger tree.

Leonardo da Vinci was similarly a kind of flower that grew on a very specific tree that was rooted in a specific time and place. During his initial years in Florence, Leonardo assisted Verrocchio on various projects, but as he matured, he eventually established his own studio in the city. His active involvement in the artistic community led to his membership in the garden of San Marcos, where he enjoyed the patronage of

Lorenzo de Medici and completed a commission for the San Donato Scopeto church.

Despite his successes in Florence, Leonardo's life took a significant turn when he decided to leave for Milan. The move was prompted by two key factors: the opportunity to work under the patronage of Ludovico Sforza, the new Duke of Milan, and allegations of sodomy, which forced him to depart Florence. This transition marked a turning point in Leonardo's career, as he blossomed into a legendary figure in Milan, producing masterpieces that would define the Renaissance era.

Moreover, in the competitive environment of Renaissance Florence, Leonardo found himself in a notable rivalry with Michelangelo. The intense competition between these two iconic artists, marked by mutual disdain, played a crucial role in pushing them to achieve artistic excellence. This rivalry, while characterized by personal animosity, reflected a broader historical pattern where competitors often turned into collaborators, contributing to the rich artistic tapestry of the time.

Eric Weiner discusses the central question he faced when writing his book *The Geography of Genius: How to Define Genius*. He presents his unconventional definition, asserting that genius is essentially a social consensus—it is someone who society collectively agrees is a genius.

Weiner emphasizes that the common debate about whether genius is innate (born) or developed (made) oversimplifies the concept. He leans toward the idea that genius is *grown*, rejecting the notion that it's solely a result of genetics. While he acknowledges the importance of hard work in developing geniuses, he argues that it doesn't fully explain the phenomenon of "genius clusters" in certain places and times.

To support his argument, Weiner cites examples such as Mozart, who exhibited prodigious talent at a young age. Despite this early display of brilliance, Weiner suggests that genetics plays only a small role in the overall genius puzzle. Instead, he posits that specifically the environment and cultural context of certain locations like Renaissance Florence, classical Athens, or contemporary Silicon Valley (where fifty percent of startups are created by people who are foreign born) contribute significantly to the concentration of geniuses in those areas.

Crucially, the ideal environment is not necessarily one of ease, wealth, or abundance. To the contrary, Weiner claims that, "One of the biggest misperceptions about places of genius, I'm discovering, is that they are akin to paradise. They are not. Paradise is antithetical to genius. Paradise makes no demands, and creative genius takes root through meeting demands in new and imaginative ways. 'The Athenians matured because they were challenged on all fronts,' said Nietzsche, in a variation of his famous 'what doesn't kill you will make you stronger' line." In other words, it was productive rivalry, and not easy fame and unquestioning support, that spurred da Vinci on to greatness.

In an interview Paul Solman concluded that for Eric Weiner, the final ingredients of genius seem pretty clear: a rich city with **bustle, competition, cooperation, and, above all, openness to the new, the foreign**. This may pose something of a mindset shift for those looking to develop their potential: The project of genius is not a purely individualistic and private one, but rather something like a co-creation that emerges from something bigger.

Now, the Renaissance is over (and not everyone agrees that it was a golden age!), but there is a lot we can take from our understanding of the period when it comes to creating our own optimal learning environments.

Cultivate a Diverse and Open Environment

Look for places that embrace diversity and openness to new ideas. Genius often thrives in cosmopolitan and culturally rich environments. Cities like ancient Athens and Vienna, which welcomed foreigners and immigrants, provided a melting pot of ideas and perspectives. Seek communities where people from different backgrounds and disciplines can interact, fostering a culture of collaboration, competition, and exchanging ideas.

This can be rather difficult in the modern world, where polarization, extremism, and intolerance of anything outside the dominant ideology abounds. As you look for this kind of environment, realize that you are also able to actively cultivate it yourself. Try to buck the trend of seeking only those who are already like yourself, and instead prioritize fruitful communication and interaction over agreement.

Prioritize Competition and Cooperation

Consider environments that strike a balance between healthy competition and cooperation. Genius clusters, such as Renaissance Florence, were competitive spaces where individuals like Leonardo da Vinci and Michelangelo pushed each other to excel. There was also cooperation and the sharing of ideas, however. Look for places that encourage both friendly competition and a collaborative spirit, creating an atmosphere that challenges individuals to reach their full potential.

There is much to say on this point, but it comes down to a wholesome spirit of collaboration that emerges out of struggle and opposition. The attitude will be your own as much as it is others'. The masters of old envisioned their work as their ultimate source and goal. A fellow artist may be your competition, but they were ultimately laboring under the same universal masters of truth and beauty and were therefore always due a certain degree of respect and fellowship.

Try to seek out and genuinely consider critique and feedback. Realize that even your enemies are your teachers, since they can help you evolve to standards of excellence far higher than a well-meaning friend might.

Embrace Interdisciplinarity and Innovation

Choose settings that encourage interdisciplinary thinking and innovation. The "Renaissance man" was not a specialist, but a fully developed and rounded human being. Even today, a "classical" education has hints of the earlier model that considered a compete education to be one that included languages, civics, physical training, music, philosophy, mathematics, natural sciences, oration, and more. Weiner believes that "today we have pigeonholed ourselves so much, that it's hard to break out. It's hard for a biologist to write about physics. It's hard for an art historian to talk about aeronautical engineering." This definitely wasn't the case in da Vinci's era.

On an individual level, what we call genius often emerges when individuals cross boundaries and investigate ideas that span a variety of fields. It is a relatively modern tendency to break down knowledge into subjects whose experts are unintelligible to one another; the Renaissance thinkers excelled because they did not see the world divided up in this way, and sought theories and innovations that were more holistic and total.

Seek places that break down silos, allowing for the exchange of ideas between different disciplines. The Viennese coffee houses, for example, were so-called "third places" that facilitated conversations between people with diverse viewpoints (fueled, no doubt, by rather a lot of caffeine!). Find environments that promote the mixing of ideas and perspectives, fostering a dynamic and innovative atmosphere.

Be Curious about Outsiders . . . Or Be One Yourself

Weiner says, "Someone who is fully invested in the status quo is not going to be a genius. They're not going to rock the boat. They're almost always outsiders. But I want to say they're not fully outsiders. They're what I call insider-outsiders."

It makes sense that if you are curious in the new, the different, and the progressive, the best people to consult are those who are able to view the dominant culture from the outside, i.e., with enough distance to gain a different insight on what is taken for granted. Try to meet with people who are "originals" and genuinely countercultural, or else find ways to explore that otherness in yourself.

The people we encounter, the conversations we have, and the narratives we immerse ourselves in have immense power to either limit or expand our own perception. Be mindful of the people you interact with, the media you consume, the build environment you engage with, and the social narratives you're enmeshed with. The name of the game is not diversity for its own sake, but fruitful conversation—even if that means sparks fly!

Weiner explains, "Almost all of these genius clusters throughout history have been cities. And Athens wasn't a huge city, but it was very dense, there were lots of interactions, and it was an urban life that we might recognize today, people trading and gossiping and getting together for these drunken symposia where they would recite poetry and drink wine." But you don't have to literally move to a big city (or get drunk on wine) to achieve similar results. Today the internet allows us access to people from all over the world. This requires extra discernment but can be an effective way to build networks that exceed those that were ever possible in the past.

Depending on your goals and what you're trying to learn, ask yourself where the physical epicenter of your craft/industry/field is. Who are the key players, and where are they? If genius is a collaborative effort, then it makes sense to think about not just your literal environment but your social environment too. Your mentor or teacher, for example, may help you make those important connections, but perhaps even more importantly, knowing the right people can allow you to start taking in some of the *zeitgeist* of your chosen field. Connect with other students, teachers who aren't your own, and also any important "nodes" in the social network. Weiner makes a direct comparison with fashion; there are fashions in intellectual circles, in industry, in tech, in art, in the hard sciences, in journalism, *everywhere*. Likewise, there are people who are trendsetters and key players; in your field, who are they?

Now, this vision of genius may seem a little discouraging. In many ways it directly contradicts the "lone genius" archetype so prevalent in modern mythology in the West. You're probably well acquainted with this story by now, as it's been played out so heavily in popular media: the genius, we are told, is someone who comes into the world with his intelligence and talent already fully installed. They achieve with ease and in complete isolation, mostly to impress and intimidate others. Their success is merely a question of them being recognized and rewarded, a process that is inevitable and requires little effort on the part of the genius. The modern-day genius, in other words, is a solitary superstar, a kind of celebrity.

The story may in fact be the complete opposite of this. If we take the Renaissance era as our model, the many geniuses produced during this era were part of clusters and groups and networks, all mutually sharing and cross-pollinating ideas, competing, collaborating, and sometimes outright battling one another. Their genius is one they cultivated slowly, bit by bit, as a product of social engagement and fruitful dialogue. Their path was complicated but virtuous. The classical genius, then, is a hero in the more traditional sense—a flower blooming on the tree, but one that would nevertheless not have existed without the tree.

Once you have found a suitable mentor (or mentors) to guide you on your path, pay some attention to your overall social and cultural environment. Think about your goals when it comes to the skill you're trying to develop, and ask about the kind of context that will be most supportive. If you cannot physically be in the ideal location, how can you access certain networks, information, or groups in other ways? If you've found the right mentor, this is precisely the kind of thing they can help you with.

Another thing to try is to identify both your rivals and your collaborators—they may be the same people! Are there other "apprentices" who are on the same path as you? Further along, perhaps? Identify them and figure out how you might start to engage them. You might find yourself spurred on by entering competitions appropriate to your level, or joining groups where you can be assured of lively back-and-forth and plenty of encouragement to do better!

Become a Renaissance Reader

"Reading maketh a full man; conference a ready man; and writing an exact man."

Francis Bacon

Your goal may be to become a language virtuoso, a better musician, a more adept painter, a free-thinking author or creative, a builder, an artisan, a crafting genius, a poet, or a master of the physical form, whether that's expressed in dance, martial arts, or feats of physical endurance. No matter what you're trying to accomplish, however, one thing is clear: Reading will help you do it better. Yes, even the martial arts!

Leonardo da Vinci was famous for his painting, but he was also extremely accomplished as a scientist, sculptor, draughtsman, inventor, architect, and general theorist. He is widely considered the world's first true "Renaissance man" and the standard for what we now consider a polymath—a person considered to have knowledge that widely spans many different areas. The word polymath comes to us from the Greek πολυμαθής or *polymathēs*, with "poly" meaning much or many and "*mathēs*" meaning learning.

It's not at all a coincidence that every individual who is considered a polymath is also a person known to be an avid—even obsessive—reader of the written word. In fact, it's hard to imagine a person "having learned much" without access to books. Da Vinci's thirst for knowledge led him to build a substantial collection of books. He benefited from the very recent invention of printing in Germany, coincidentally sharing the same age as the printing press—another hint about the nature of the "genius clusters" that so fascinated Weiner. In da Vinci's time, however, many books were still hand-copied and astonishingly precious.

But da Vinci didn't only consume the written word; he produced it, too. When he passed away at the age of sixty-seven, he left behind an extensive legacy of over six thousand pages of notebooks. These notebooks contained a wealth of content, including anatomical studies, military inventions, sketches of nature, and notes derived from the books he'd accessed in various libraries. This gives us a hint not only of the size of his love for books, but of his character. This was not a man who "collected" books for their own sake, admiring the aesthetics of a well-coordinated bookshelf or reading the Renaissance version of the bestseller list just because it was popular. Rather, books were instrumental. They served a very specific purpose in the life of the polymath.

Being a Renaissance reader involved a different approach to reading compared to modern readers. During the Renaissance, the printing press revolutionized book production, making books more affordable and accessible. This accessibility, however, comes with a downside, as the sheer volume of available books creates a certain "noise" in the literary world. In contrast to the modern reader, who faces an overwhelming abundance of choices, a Renaissance reader like Leonardo had a more limited selection . . . but what he had access to was almost always of exceptional quality. Fewer people were literate, and the barrier to entry for publishing a work was extremely high. No book was published unless it demonstrably added to what came before.

This meant that although books were costly and relatively scarce, they were of an entirely different quality. The world of mass paperback printing and high volume but disposable entertainment reading was many decades to come. Instead, a reader could expect to encounter material that was serious, rich, rarified, and intended for audiences who possessed the patience, education, and intellectual sophistication to make real use of what they found in those pages. To illustrate this point nicely, consider that da Vinci considered himself a "man without learning" and strived continually to learn new languages, filling his library with dictionaries and grammar books to better access the knowledge he felt he lacked. Standards, in other words, were sky-high.

Books would have been read slowly, carefully, and patiently, and often re-read again and again. Diligent students were expected to know Latin and maybe a little Greek, and learning in a completely different language was par for the course. Well-formed and elegant handwriting was non-negotiable, and students of all kinds were expected to have exceptional memories and recite vast tracts of text by heart—an achievement almost unimaginable to modern man. Reading was not a passive activity, but an extension of what was seen as the ultimate learning format: conversation. The student was thus always in *dialogue* with the material that they read and would actively engage by taking notes, writing rebuttals, and composing letters and other responses (the author may indeed be known in their social circle).

Da Vinci's biographer Walter Isaacson explained how books and notebooks became a kind of external brain and a way to process and shape certain paths of learning. The young Leonardo would watch wild birds for hours on end, but then he would sit down and recreate what he had seen and learned on the pages of his notebook, sketching out the designs of their wings, allowing that architecture to settle into his brain and develop into new ideas. In fact, he sketched his famous *Vitruvian Man* in this co-creative manner: He studied the works of the famous Vitruvius, who was an ancient Roman architect and civil engineer, and then designed a kind of pictorial response, both expressing his understanding of the work but simultaneously expanding it. Books, then, were a powerful technology that enabled the educated man to converse, as it were, with people from different times and places so that new ideas and understandings could be generated, then shared again.

On da Vinci's bookshelf you might have found hand-drawn maps from famous cartographers and explorers, a printing of *Aesop's Fables*, *The Divine Comedy* (in Italian, of course), Ovid's *Metamorphoses*, richly illustrated anatomy and medical texts, a few Latin dictionaries, a book by Benedetto de l'Abaco, who instituted the use of Arabic numerals, many mathematical treatises, illuminated religious manuscripts (both original and copied), and many major and minor works on botany, hydraulics, mechanics, and cosmology. If you wanted to emulate the great polymaths of old, there is surely a lesson here: Strive to have a bookshelf that makes you hard to categorize!

With da Vinci as our model, how can we go about planning our own self-education on those well-traveled paths of the printed word? First and most importantly, this style of reading is not so much a *what* as it is a *how*. The reading is a means to an end—what matters is the active and curious engagement of knowledge and its mechanisms; it just so happens that reading and writing are one of the most effective tools we have for this kind of intellectual activity.

Let's take a look at some ways to embody the Renaissance approach to our own reading:

Design Your Reading Environment

Reading is a lifelong activity. It should play a permanent and central role in your life, whatever your chosen disciplines and subjects. That means that it should be built into your daily routine along with everything else you do almost automatically. Depending on your resources, consider investing in a proper desk, a suitable light source, and other accessories that enhance your focus and comfort during reading sessions. The more your reading space inspires and welcomes you, the more at home you'll feel there. Can you include easy access to pens, paper, notebooks, and other items to help you engage with your material? Depending on your subject, you might like to invest in a few pieces of stationery to help you stay organized, such as shelves, files, folders, highlighters, corkboards, sticky notes, and so on.

Classical paintings from this era show lush studios and drawing rooms that were as much works of art as they were practical learning spaces. A common practice was to place a skull on the desk—a memento mori—or other religious items or decorative knickknacks from far-off places to denote prestige or bring some beauty, mysticism, or inspiration to the space. You can follow suit by decorating your space in a way that reaffirms your own goals and intentions, as well as motivates you to keep pushing onward. Some simple ideas include beautiful pictures and paintings, trophies and certificates, "vision boards," photos of loved ones, moving quotes and poetry, or symbolic ornaments that speak to your purpose.

Actively Engage with the Text

Now on to the actual reading. Renaissance readers *actively engaged* with texts by having a pen in hand. Reading was a part of thinking—it was something you absorbed, digested, processed, and responded to. Men of learning from this period, da Vinci included, marked up texts to fully comprehend meanings and implications. It was as though the author were right there in the room with them, delivering a lecture they fully intended the audience to stop and ask them questions about.

Take notes, underline key passages, and interact with the text while reading. Consider keeping a *commonplace book* or learning notebook to collect and organize important information for future reference. For da Vinci, this was a multimedia affair and contained snippets of verse, drawings, designs for inventions, and more. For the modern reader, you can keep your questions, objections, and responses either in a notebook or typed up on a computer. We will be looking more at exactly how to take effective notes in a later chapter, but the most effective method will always be the one you devise for yourself, since it will fit your life, your goals, and your needs perfectly.

Have Both a Practical and an Intellectual Goal

Much later on, as literacy rates climbed and reading became more popular, things like novels abounded and more and more ordinary people had access to material of all kinds, not just heavyweight academic manuscripts. It became possible to read simply for entertainment or even distraction.

During the Renaissance era, this attitude would have seemed absurd. Instead, reading was done with a purpose. Every intellectual effort was aimed at some definite practical or intellectual goals—usually a mix of both, and only the extremely idle elite would attempt an education merely as an ornament to courtly life and not truly intended to be put to use.

Today, the sheer volume of information out there means that no human being can process it within a single lifetime; this means that you are necessarily limited and must choose. Goals are a way to focus and prioritize. They help you chart a route through the noise and distraction. If you understand *why* you are reading before you even pick up a book, your attention will be more alive and targeted than if you had read with no special aim in particular. Whether it's for academic, professional, or personal reasons, read with the intention of using the knowledge gained. Go in with unanswered questions, and let your curiosity bring the words to life for you.

Some additional things to try:

Actively consider how the material can be applied or incorporated into your own work and thinking. It may apply to a completely different area than the one you're investigating. Make a note, make connections, and follow up later.

Write your questions in the margins as you read. Alternatively, pause now and then to digest what you've read and guess what will be said next. This way you are teaching yourself to not just read, but "think along with" the author. You will gain so much more insight this way. Similarly, express your disagreement or concerns in the margins, too. Have you read a counterargument to this one? Where? Weigh it all up.

Get into the habit of skimming and scanning before you read in depth. Look at the titles and subtitles, labels or diagrams, graphs, and so on. Try to understand a piece in the broadest terms first, then dig in, summarizing each section and even paragraph for its main point.

Read bibliographies. Follow references made by authors you like to see who *they* are reading. It's not going to recreate Renaissance Europe, but it's a surprisingly effective way to enter into certain ideological networks where you can really begin to grasp more wide-reaching themes.

Summary:

- Leonardo da Vinci was a Renaissance-era polymath, painter, inventor, scientist, artisan, draughtsman, philosopher, botanist, sculptor, and musician. By studying his life and philosophy, we can imbue our own lives with a little of his famous curiosity.
- The first step is to secure an appropriate mentor. Born to humble beginnings, da Vinci was self-taught and apprenticed himself at the age of fourteen to a master painter who tutored him. He was diligent and deferred to

him in all things, understanding the importance of consistent practice and training.
- Follow the correct mentoring process, beginning with deep observation (passive mode), then skills acquisition (practice mode), and finally experimentation (active mode).
- A good mentor should be a genuine expert in their field, know how to get the most from their students, and not be threatened if the student surpasses them. They should be able to demonstrate open-mindedness to approaches other than their own and be able to point to past students who have excelled.
- Be mindful of your environment, which is also a kind of tutor, influencing the character and development of your thought. Seek a diverse and open environment where bustle, competition, cooperation, newness, and difference are the norm. Be welcoming to outsiders and outsider thought, embracing interdisciplinarity with others unlike yourself. Find ways to collaborate and connect.
- To be a Renaissance reader, develop a consistent habit of both reading and note-taking. Build daily routines based in a well-crafted learning environment, and actively engage with the text, continually comparing

it against your goals and intentions. Read widely, diligently, and strategically ... and do it every single day.

Chapter 2: The Mind of the Polymath

The Heart of All Learning

"I would rather have questions that can't be answered than answers that can't be questioned."

Richard P. Feynman

Hopefully, you are now on your way to securing a mentor or teacher for yourself, have started to read and gradually build up your own library of books and notes, and have started paying attention to the environment around you. As you consider your own goals, you may have come up against a pretty fundamental question: Why do any of this?

Why learn ballet or ancient Japanese calligraphy or maritime history of New England in the first place?

In the last chapter, we took steps to build a foundation onto which we can begin to build a learning life. Now the question arises: How will we build on that foundation? In this chapter, we'll be considering the most fundamental traits required of a lifelong learner—and they are not tools, but rather *attitudes*.

As you'll soon see, da Vinci and others like him were intelligent, but they were also masters at cultivating the mindset required to genuinely discover or create something new in their worlds. It may just be the mindset that makes the real difference, and not the intelligence. What exactly is the mindset required? Arguably the most important characteristic is **curiosity**.

Da Vinci demonstrated an insatiable intellectual appetite that spanned diverse disciplines, including architecture, anatomy, aeronautics, and robotics. Despite his wide-ranging talents, da Vinci also found success in theatrical production, notably designing lavish festivals in Florence and Milan. Unashamed of his curiosity and operating in a child-like fantasy world, he prioritized safety, appreciation, and the freedom to explore over financial gain, creating not for others but to satisfy his intellectual hunger. Unbound by formal education, he relied on acute visual thinking, seamlessly integrating groundbreaking scientific studies into his artwork and vice versa, contributing to his exceptional versatility.

Compared to the business moguls and tech billionaires who pass for genius in our modern era, da Vinci was called to something higher than financial gain or market domination. He learned because he genuinely, sincerely *wanted to know*. His curiosity was underpinned by a keen power of observation, sparking profound explorations that evolved into marvelous creativity. Flamboyant, authentic, and unabashedly alternative, he embraced his uniqueness, exhibiting a secure and self-assured demeanor. His self-reflective nature led to copious journal writings, capturing thoughts, frustrations, and ongoing projects. These notes fueled his self-discovery and self-development, providing insights into his creative process and leaving behind a rich legacy for future generations to study and admire.

His life's work was colorful, rich, and lively. And it all started with curiosity. Why were birds' wings shaped the way they were? Could it be possible for water to flow uphill? What is truth? What is beauty? If I put a rudder on the bottom of this thing here, will it stop it from tipping over? What is Neptune made of on the inside?

Cultivating Intense da Vincian Curiosity
Da Vinci lived in a curious age, and he was both the cause and result of a period of intense intellectual growth. Our own era by comparison is stifled; those who would learn can often see no greater end purpose than perhaps "disrupting" some industry to eke out a narrow margin of profit, or acquiring a skill for the sole purpose of increasing hireability in a hostile market. Creativity is seldom more than the recombination of tired tropes, and knowledge is demoted to mere "data"—cheap information in enormous quantities that nevertheless amounts to little.

Leonardo da Vinci fostered an intense curiosity about people and the world around him. He knew how to ask questions to get interesting answers, utilizing the information to inspire his inventions and creations. Da Vinci meticulously documented his inquiries and observations in numerous notebooks, chronicling days spent exploring the countryside in a quest for understanding. His curiosity delved into diverse subjects, such as the existence of shells on mountaintops, the immediate visibility of lightning compared to the delayed sound of thunder, and the mechanics of how a bird sustains itself in flight.

Da Vinci, as described by scholar Michael Gelb, extensively studied and sketched flowers and plants from various perspectives to gain a comprehensive understanding of their anatomy. In a journal entry, da Vinci expressed his fascination with the multitude of actions humans perform, the diversity of animals, trees, plants, and flowers, and the variety in landscapes, architecture, instruments, costumes, ornaments, and arts.

Beyond botany and nature, da Vinci applied his intense curiosity to his artistic creations by examining paintings through a mirror. This reflective practice aimed to enable a more objective assessment of the strengths and weaknesses of his artworks. This, in effect, is what curiosity is: looking at familiar things, but backward, in an attempt to see them as they really are, to see them as they are without our assumptions and foregone conclusions.

But what does curiosity look like in the internet age?

Is it possible to cultivate a little of that same attitude today, in a vastly different world to the one da Vinci inhabited?

The answer is yes! It does, however, take a mindset shift. Da Vinci was a genius because of what he *didn't* know. He went out in search not of questions that he could easily answer, but of those that stumped him, challenged him, and demanded much patience and diligence to answer. What we can learn from this approach is that true genius is not about ease and accomplishment. Rather, it's about the *process* of uncovering knowledge, and the journey from ignorance to understanding. That process isn't always neat, pretty, or comfortable.

The person who is uneasy with mystery cannot embrace it long enough to learn from it. The person who is too egotistical to admit they don't know, or too proud to ask a simple question, will never have the privilege of learning or having that simple question answered (and it's the simple ones that are often the deepest and most mysterious of all!).

One foolproof technique is to follow da Vinci's reported childlike nature and do what all children naturally do: ask loads of questions. The man asked questions of himself, of others, of the books he wrote, of nature itself. He was not automatically satisfied by the easy, conventional answers of the day, either, and kept interrogating. *Why* was such-and-so the case?

In Michael Gelb's book *How to Think Like a Da Vinci*, he suggests the following exercise to practice formulating great questions:

1. Try to make a list of the one hundred questions that are most important to you in one sitting. Then, go back through the list and look for themes. What are most of your questions actually about?
2. Now, choose ten questions that are most important to you and rank them in importance. These questions should relate to your broad quality of life. Remember, learning should be focused on a goal or purpose.
3. Next, develop ten questions from your professional field about your career or some other aspect of your professional life. Don't be afraid to ask the simple questions, since they're often the most profound.

You can also take a page out of esteemed Richard Feynman's book and compile your own list of twelve burning questions—things that you are truly, almost maddeningly curious about. Compiling and regularly updating this list not only keeps you focused and "on purpose," but it also allows you to uncover interesting areas of overlap between seemingly disparate areas. Renaissance thinkers were looking for big ideas that encapsulated all subjects. If you look at your list, can you find what connects two seemingly unrelated questions?

Finally, one useful technique is to actively welcome your mistakes and convert them into questions that will help you learn. If you failed at something, ask why and be genuinely open to learning the answer. Rather than enjoying the knowledge you're accumulating, look more closely at the gaps and what you are currently ignorant of, or else the assumptions you are making. If you have a blind spot, how can you address the issue? Who can you ask? If you don't have the answer, then where might it be?

Having an open, receptive mindset means accepting that fumbling in the dark is a big part of being a creator, inventor, scientist, and thinker. Start with your own pet theories and biases. Do you have quality evidence for your various beliefs and theories? Challenge yourself if nobody else will challenge you—make your ideas earn their keep! Remember, too, that just because you don't know something now, it doesn't mean that you can't learn it. Lacking a skill today doesn't mean you will lack it forever. Just be curious about the next step. Learn a little every day, fine-tune your skill one step at a time, and you cannot help but learn.

The Right Attitude

Though it's probably going too far to suggest that Renaissance-era polymaths possessed a certain type of personality, it is true that they conducted themselves in remarkably similar ways—in other words, their approach to life was predictable.

Idea 1: Learning never ends

Commit to continuous learning. We develop not so that we can arrive at the end of our development. We continue on—one horizon, once reached, opens up to another. There's no doubt that had da Vinci lived longer than his almost seventy years, he would have continued to learn and create. What's required is that we don't get too comfortable in what we already know, what we've already achieved, and the skills we've already acquired. Instead, we need to keep learning alive by asking what remains unknown, unachieved, and unacquired.

Idea 2: Test out your theories in the real world

Apply everything you learn, develop, or create to the real world and the practical goals you have there. It can be a trap to get lost in abstraction; instead, continually see how your predictions and ideas measure up against reality. Do they work? How do they compare to what's currently out there? How can you test and improve on what you've done? Experience is a master teacher, if you're courageous enough to embrace your mistakes and failures.

Idea 3: Embrace the unknown

Da Vinci was a man of science and learning, but he was also a Catholic and a "spiritual metaphysician" who would have embedded all his learning in a framework wherein God was the master mathematician, artist, and architect of the universe itself. All this is to say that for a man like da Vinci, the world was not a machine to be broken into parts and coldly analyzed, but a beautiful mystery. Great thinkers of old had a depth and nobility of soul that helped them understand the value of the mysterious and the enigmatic.

Practically speaking, this meant that their curiosity was often tinged with awe, respect, and wonder. They were comfortable with ambiguity and could endure paradox and contradiction for a long time as they chiseled away at problems, trying to grasp their deeper meaning. Uncertainty, then, is not an enemy to be destroyed but something that is always beckoning, something to relish and appreciate.

Idea 4: Be humble

Learning is about the privilege of knowing the previously unknown and seeing the previously unseen; it's not about the glory and vanity of being the knower or the seer.

Being humble has practical value, too. Those people who are best able to move past mistakes, faulty assumptions, outright failures, and wrong turns are the ones who are quickest to get on with the real work of doing better. Ego and pride only get in the way—bearing in mind that feeling down on yourself or overly pessimistic is a kind of vanity, too! If something is difficult or beyond you, don't give up simply because it's a little humiliating to be confronted with evidence of your limitations.

If you receive a correction or critical feedback, realize that there's nothing to be ashamed of and nothing to defend against. Da Vinci and many others like him were fantastically wrong about more things than the average human being. The trick is to see far beyond "right" and "wrong" and simply become curious about what *is*.

The Elastic Mind

"The measure of intelligence is the ability to change."

Albert Einstein

Because mindset is the first and most important tool in the lifelong learner's kit, we'll spend a little longer exploring exactly what this attitude is and how you can cultivate it in your own life. To do this, we'll consider a physiological metaphor. Think about the physical world you live in, your body, and the way these two things interact. Your body (or the body of another person or even an animal or plant) is successful in as much as it can respond to its environment, navigate it successfully, overcome the challenges it poses, and to the extent possible, master it. Such bodies tend to have qualities that reflect their environments—the body is a manifest physical *response* to the environment.

Now, our mind can be considered another kind of organ or entity, and one that engages in the same way, only with a different aspect of the environment. Just as an organism's body adopts the shape that will best allow it to survive and adapt to its surroundings, the mind of a human being allows them to survive and adapt to the hidden underlying realities beyond the physical world—its patterns of organization, its laws, its more fundamental principles, its connections.

Every animal, and every organ in every animal, is considered healthy and adaptive when it is strong, flexible, and responsive to its environment. A healthy mind follows the same principle: It expresses its full potential when it is **strong, flexible, and responsive to its environment**.

What is the world we inhabit? It is ever-changing, complex, rich, and filled with mystery. It presents some aspects to us while concealing others. It responds to our actions but also acts on us. Given all this, what does the ideal mind look like? Well, that's easy: It's one that is able to adapt to change, able to grasp and work with complexity, comfortable with depth and richness, and tolerant of—even grateful for—hidden mystery. It's certainly one that can quickly change plans, recover from adversity, and try something new.

Elastic thinking, then, is a property of a healthy mind. In nature, things that are stiff or brittle, things that are stubborn, and things that are unable to respond and adapt to the flow of change end up getting washed away with that change. One could even say that life itself is characterized by this movement, this responsiveness, and this flow. To be fixed and unmoving, to fail to be in dynamic dialogue with reality—this is pretty close to being dead or inanimate!

A mind that is flexible is one that can reinvent itself over and over again. Considering that the Renaissance literally means "rebirth," we can see how this characteristic is built into da Vinci's historical period. With mental elasticity, we can be new, think new. We can shift perspective, solve problems, create tools, cultivate beauty, devise models. We can see into what is currently not working, and possess enough imagination to try out something else.

In this view, then, growth is the same as learning is the same as flexibility. Look at a tree—the growing parts are at the very edge of the plant, at the vanguard, and reaching hopefully out into the unknown. These parts are most alive, but they are also the most tender, new, and flexible. This is the leading edge where innovation, exploration, creativity, and novelty all blend into one. The hard wood of the tree's trunk is relatively static and unchanging. This represents banked knowledge and wisdom, convention, tradition, logic, and order. It is not that growth requires that we routinely destroy what has come before due to a mad addiction to novelty; rather, we continuously grow on what has come before.

Leonard Mlodinow is a theoretical physicist and author of *Elastic: Flexible Thinking in a Time of Change*. In his book, he explains, "Logical analytical thinking is really good when you are trying to solve a problem you've seen before. You can use known methods and techniques to approach whatever issue you are dealing with. Elastic thinking is what you need when the circumstances change, and you are dealing with something new. It's not about following rules."

Leonardo da Vinci definitely possessed an elastic mind. His genius was not merely a product of innate talent but stemmed from his wildly imaginative, curious, and unwaveringly adaptable nature. His deliberate cultivation of novelty through his own will and effort makes his story inspirational but also possible for others to realistically emulate.

Other traits of the elastically minded include:

- The capacity to let go of comfortable ideas and admit when they're wrong.
- Tolerance of ambiguity and contradiction. This includes the patience required to wait while things are unresolved or still in process.
- The courage to rise above conventional mindsets—something increasingly difficult

to do given our current intellectual monoculture.
- Being able to switch perspectives, view an idea from many angles, and have empathy for others unlike themselves (yes, there are as many ways to think as there are thinkers!).
- Knowing how to reframe questions, tweak the tools we're using, and adjust our methods.
- The intellectual honesty to challenge ingrained assumptions—not others', but our own.
- Knowing how to rely on imagination as much as logic and to cultivate a complete and holistic intellect rather than to heavily focus on one area to the detriment of another.
- The willingness to experiment and to be surprised by what one discovers.
- Tolerance of failure and the ability to gracefully process an unexpected result.
- The skill to generate a variety of ideas and integrate them with others—essentially, the ability to tell stories and construct larger narratives and theories.

Let's be realistic, these characteristics are not going to be completely developed by completing an easy one-week YouTube course or reading a cute pop science book released by a big publishing house. Some people come into the world with a fair bit of this personality trait already in place, but for most of us, it will be a lifetime's work to properly cultivate the correct *intellectual posture* in the face of the unknown. Luckily, a lifetime is exactly how much time we have, so we might as well start right now! Here are some ideas.

Develop Neophilia—i.e., Embrace Novelty

Actively seek out and expose yourself to new concepts, industries, and perspectives regularly. This could involve reading articles from various fields, attending varied events, or joining communities outside your usual social circles. When you encounter someone with a very different background, perspective, or approach, lean in and try to learn more about them rather than giving in to the human reflex to automatically assume that they're wrong.

Explore different forms of art or media that you wouldn't typically encounter. Keep asking, in whatever way you can, "What's out there for me? What's going on?" Be willing to fall down a few rabbit holes! This can stimulate creativity and encourage you to see connections between seemingly unrelated concepts.

Deliberately Allocate Time for Daydreaming and Reflection

Even though it probably annoyed his patrons and employers, da Vinci was known for taking long breaks from painting *The Last Supper*. Then again, he would also paint for long stretches of time, but likely only after his creative juices had been given time to replenish. The mind, just like the organs and tissues of the body, has its limits and needs to rest and recharge if it hopes to function optimally. "All work and no play" is not really a concept that fits into the Renaissance thinker's worldview—because the best work feels like play, and the most fascinating play can often lead to the deepest work. Give your mind the space to wander and make connections between unrelated ideas. This unstructured thinking time can lead to innovative thoughts and solutions.

The trick is, however, to allow genuine empty space and rest time in your life. The "power nap" is an oxymoron created by Silicon Valley types who are deathly afraid of inactivity. Remember that an effort to relax is a failure to relax if you are filling up your "downtime" with a complicated regime of breathing exercises and meditation goals—you're not resting at all. Integrate deliberate pauses in your day for unfocused thinking. Doodle and dawdle along, see where your nose takes you, tinker with this and that, slob around, or do nothing in particular.

These "negative space goals" allow your mind to wander and may lead to unexpected connections and creative breakthroughs (but, of course, that is not their *purpose*, so don't sit quietly on the periphery and wait like a hunter in the grass for a big eureka moment. Rest is sufficient in itself and is its own reward).

Embrace the Unconventional

This one is far more than mere rebelliousness. It is not enough to simply push back against anything you perceive as established. Rather, it's about looking at things with fresh eyes. Actively seek out ideas or concepts that you disagree with—realizing that this is not the same as repeatedly playing out the same rote arguments in your head where you prove to yourself how right you are to think as you do!

Understand the arguments supporting these ideas, and the motivations behind them. Practice intellectual empathy in the sense that you consider certain ideas and theories not from within your worldview, but from within someone else's. Don't merely entertain an idea, but become curious about the mind and context out of which that idea sprang. What purpose does it serve? How does it show up the limitations and assumptions in your own set of mental circumstances? This practice helps you develop a more nuanced and flexible mindset.

Don't be afraid to question established norms and explore unconventional solutions, but again, be discerning about how you're going to define "conventional" in the first place. Your task is not to clearly identify what the dominant ideology has agreed upon as conventional. Your task is to look closely at the dominant ideology itself. You'll know you're doing this right if this feels extremely difficult!

It's not necessary to reinvent the wheel each time and delve all the way into deconstruction and analysis—some rabbit holes go too deep, after all. It's enough, however, to simply get in the habit of second-guessing your first impulse, your assumption, and what your environment has taken as a set of givens. Remember, the goal is to shift from top-down analytical thinking to bottom-up elastic thinking, allowing your mind to stretch beyond familiar boundaries and adapt to new challenges. If you are only mimicking the route taken by your culture's current celebrated innovators and heroes, you're likely already a decade out of date. *New solutions, by definition, will not look like old new solutions.*

Don't Throw Out the Old

Recall the growing tree and the way that the tender new buds depend on the solid, unmoving trunk beneath to support them. Recall how many years da Vinci had to dedicate to learning the rules before he broke them. Innovation and novelty are valuable, but they need to be tempered with a respect for what all this novelty should be grounded in.

Leonard Mlodinow warns that elastic thinking on its own can be akin to chaos and craziness.

Remember that a healthy mind is strong, flexible, and responsive to the environment—sometimes, the environment demands we stop, consolidate, and proceed logically through a series of concrete steps we are already familiar with. "If you are one hundred percent on the elastic side," says Mlodinow, "and you have no executive function of your brain ordering your thoughts, you will end up non-functional. The ideas will come so fast and so disconnected you can never get anything done." In other words, you'll quickly become that unflattering "nutty professor" archetype who doesn't get anything done.

Try thinking of the learning process as a series of inhalations and exhalations. Breathing in is, literally, like inspiration, and you bring in new concepts, fresh ideas, and unusual possibilities, expanding yourself. But an inhalation is followed by an exhalation. Whatever you learn can be consolidated by seeing how it connects to what you already know. How can it be applied? Can it be applied, for that matter, or is it better discarded? Adjust as you go so that on the next inhale, you are ready to take in some more fresh novelty. This way, rest and effort, new and old, logical and creative are balanced and play off one another. We will explore this concept of balance a little more in our final chapter.

Sensazione

The modern-day concept of an overly cerebral nerdy type would not have made much sense to the Renaissance men of da Vinci's era. Just as it was with their classical forebears, a successful human being was at the time understood to be a *fully rounded* one, and it was seen as just as much a shame to neglect the intellect as it was to neglect the body and its development.

Your chosen field of development may focus on the body and its sense perceptions, but chances are you are one of the many people who associates learning with the sedentary, internal, cognitive realm, and not with the workings of the flesh, blood, and nerves.

Michael Gelb's *How to Think like Leonardo da Vinci* introduces da Vinci's sensory principle, termed *Sensazione*, which simply translates to "sensation" in Italian. The body is thus a central conduit through which learning and understanding can enter, and knowledge begins necessarily as embodied knowledge—the world as it is perceived by us through our various sense organs. This principle revolves around the continuous refinement of the senses (particularly sight, in da Vinci's case) to mediate one's experiences.

Learning, then, is not an intellectual activity supplemented by occasionally remembering that you have a body and sense organs; rather, we attempt to broaden and expand our understanding of what learning *is*, opening all possible channels so that we can receive many different forms of understanding. Our engagement with the world is thus three-dimensional, connected, and dynamic.

The Boston Museum of Science's long-running exhibit highlights how da Vinci, influenced by ancient texts, diverged from traditional approaches by actively observing nature and posing simple yet profound scientific questions. These were not dry hypotheticals but living questions. For instance, he inquired into the mechanics of bird flight and meticulously documented his findings in sketches, some of which strike the viewer today for their beauty and vital character. He did not conduct any of this work solely in writing, hunched in a study somewhere with a candle. Rather, he observed with his eyes, replicated what he saw, heard, and encountered, and engaged with what he encountered using the totality of himself.

Sight, sound, smell, taste, touch . . . when any of these is deadened, we lose an invaluable portion of experience, lose our sense of wonder and awe, and lose our ability to be surprised or even thrilled by the natural (and supernatural) world around us. As we encounter our reality, we internalize a mental picture of what it is, and this means that the way we "encode" this initial representation depends heavily on the channels through which we do it—our five senses. Gelb explains in another bestseller, *Subtle Speculation: The Art of Visualization*, that "the ability to visualize a desired outcome is built into your brain, and your brain is designed to help you succeed in matching that picture with your performance. And the more thoroughly you involve all your senses, the more compelling your visualization becomes."

There are now several compelling research studies evidencing the idea of an *ideomotor reflex*, i.e., the body's tiny but measurable physical response to what it merely imagines. When you imagine a lemon vividly enough, you salivate, but the response can be subtler than this. Beholding the movement of the bird's wings, we imagine the mechanics of flight, and in response there are tiny, imperceptible movements in the muscles of *our own* arms. There is a dance between the bird's wings, the play of light on the surface of our eyeballs, the recognition of what we're seeing, their muscles and ours, and the movement of our inner comprehension as we make meaning of it all.

Embodied perception and thinking are connected—the richer the one is, the richer the other will be. Merely reading about something produces knowledge that is flat and static. Engaging with it via your body and senses is a more fluid and holistic way of knowing. Modern people like to think that they are blessed to live in a world of informational abundance and more media than they could possibly ever consume. They may fail to see the relative "thinness" of this media and how this data is a mere reference to something in the world—it is not that thing itself.

Thus, we have the stereotype of a highly educated psychologist who is socially awkward and alienated from actual human beings and their behaviors, an ecologist who lives in a city and gives talks about the interconnectedness of life without ever once witnessing it firsthand, or an architect who is a master at two-dimensional drawings but has never felt the texture of plaster or cement against their fingertips.

Fully inhabiting your senses is closely connected with mindfulness and will increase your abilities to self-regulate, recall information, and simply enjoy each moment deeply, rather than skimming over its surface.

According to da Vinci, the person without this mindfulness "looks without seeing, listens without hearing, touches without feeling, eats without tasting, moves without physical awareness, inhales without awareness of odor or fragrance, and talks without thinking." Perhaps instead of rushing ahead in a conceited attempt to always find something new to encounter, something bigger or better or faster, we can simply train ourselves to perceive *what is already here*—all those things we may have neglected to fully comprehend in the first place. Many scientists, innovators, inventors, and artists do just this: They allow us to really see what had been there all along.

Just how sensitive can you make your organs of perception?

How refined can you make these channels of awareness?

Can we learn to not just look, but to perceive, to behold, to admire, to inquire, to peer with awed curiosity, with respectful tenderness, with interest, with joy?

What would it look like to not just passively receive from the senses, but to connect in a relational way, to dialogue with reality?

Become a Multisensory Being
Though it's easy to wax lyrical about the senses (no coincidence, is it?), it's worth remembering that this is all concrete work—poetry that is always anchored in the endless here and now and connected irreducibly to the physical forms we inhabit. Becoming a person more connected to their physical form is not difficult; it simply requires a little space into which we can become aware.

Mindfulness has been the buzzword for many years now, but the emphasis on the "mind" part does a disservice to the potential bodily richness we can bring to our awareness. Throughout the day, can you quickly "check in" with your senses (or rather, stop making the efforts to numb out or ignore that awareness)?

Can you become aware of the tone and quality of the air in the room around you? What is the feeling of the light in the sky right now, and can you trace the tiniest shifts in its hue? Listen with every ounce of attention to things around you. Precisely where is a sound coming from, and how far away? Can you replicate that exact tone in your own mind, or even hum or sing it yourself? If you're out walking and you pick a leaf, can you crush it between your fingers, sniff it with closed eyes, and let your mind tell you what it's reminded of? Can you remember the color of the front door to your friend's house? Can you tell the difference between black pepper and white pepper?

None of these questions will necessarily lead you to some profound scientific discovery or inspire a creative work of genius in you. But they don't have to. What they can do is start to sharpen your sensory awareness and bring you into a more profound and intelligent connection with the world around you. After all, how could you ever learn the difference between black and white pepper unless you literally tasted or smelled it? Try to imagine that this is the way with *all* knowledge—it becomes real for us when passed through the interface of our senses.

Here are some exercises you can practice to enhance your own sensory abilities. Don't worry if you have long thought of yourself as not having a good sense of smell or being tone deaf—the senses can be trained just like every other part of us! Try doing one or more of the following:

Eat with Your Eyes Closed

Use your sense of smell and taste to compare. You may compare two different wines or two types of chicken dishes made with slightly different spices. How small can you make the differences before your taste buds lose the ability to distinguish? Take time to appreciate the aromas and the varying tastes that hit your palate. Notice if the tastes seem to have a connection with the smells. Food is not just taste and smell, however—your tongue is touching food. What is its texture, its weight, its volume, its size, its heat, its density? What is the total experience of eating this meal? When you are done, open your eyes and look at what you created in your mind's eye and if or how it matches up with your previous expectations.

Merge Your Senses by Practicing Synesthesia

For example, draw music. Listen to your favorite concerto, opera, hip-hop, or rock tune. As you do, start to draw using crayons, markers, or paint (even finger paint!). Perhaps you can listen to one form of music and compare it to another.

Or create a drawing and then subsequently ask yourself how it might sound. What instrument best represents this shade of blue? Is a grey-toned picture of a palm tree more like a choir or a solo voice unaccompanied?

The five senses do not operate In isolation from one another. This is why most cultures agree on the connection between sensations of different types—we think that red is hot (color and touch), kindness feels sweet (emotion and taste), major scales somehow match up with happy bright colors (music and sight), and some music just stinks (sound and smell!). You'd be surprised just how much creativity and novelty spring from opening the gates between the various senses—something you necessarily cannot do if you only operate using just one sense.

Think about a problem that you might be having in your work or personal life. Give it a color, shape, or texture and imagine what it smells like or what taste it might have. Draw it out. You may even consider adding movement and emotion to the mix. Take it as far as your imagination will let you. Ask yourself what your office life would be like if it were an opera or a painting, or what your lunch would be if it were a song. If the math problem you are working on could talk, what accent would it have?

Practice Mindfulness in Nature

The Japanese love immersive forest walks so much they have their own name for the practice: *shinrin-yoku*, or forest bathing. It involves walking through a forest while emerging your senses to take in the sights, smells, sounds, tastes, or textile experience of nature to benefit your health. A form of mindfulness meditation practice, it involves being in a moment-by-moment awareness of your thoughts, sensations, and feelings, as well as of the surrounding environment. You're not in a rush to get anywhere. You're just seeing how deeply you can sink into your senses.

Before we end this chapter, one caveat is to not get hung up on how "artistic" you may or may not be. Remembering how corrosive ego can be, try to keep the performance element out of your creative exploration and engage in your senses simply for the sake of the experience—not to achieve some desired end result. The most creative among us know that the value of the artistic process is in staying open, receptive, curious, and expressive—too much self-judgment can seriously get in the way.

That means that even if you don't think you're any good at it, regularly engage in the arts. Write and read poetry, play with paints and pens and other media, cook and bake (the kitchen is a museum of fascinating aromas!), dance, practice athletics or wrestling, sing, compose little songs or write lyrics, try your hand at crafts of all kinds, experiment with design, fashion, and interiors, or buy some clay and see what your curious hands can make of it. If nothing else, it will be fun.

Summary:

- The most fundamental trait of a lifelong learner like da Vinci is an attitude of insatiable curiosity. Shift your mindset toward a focus on unanswered questions. Be childlike and continually experiment with different perspectives. Keep a running list of open questions to guide and inspire your learning.
- The right attitude is patient enough to practice learning as a lifelong pursuit, humble enough to engage with mistakes and the unknown, and practical enough to use real-world experience to inform one's mental models.
- An elastic mind is healthy in the same way that a body is healthy: It can change, and it is strong, flexible, and responsive to its environment. Where the mind is flexible and able to grow and adjust, innovation, exploration, creativity, and novelty are possible.
- Elastic thinking requires dynamism, adaptability, courage, and a love for the

unconventional—although it always anchors in the known.
- Da Vinci's principle of "sensazione" reminds us that learning should never be purely intellectual, but multisensory. Renaissance men were fully rounded and highly developed in sense perception. You can develop this capacity in yourself by slowing down, practicing synesthesia, and engrossing yourself in nature with senses fully switched on.

Chapter 3: A Map of the Intellect

Be a T-shaped Human

"The height of the pinnacle is determined by the breadth of the base."

Ralph Waldo Emerson

Leonardo Da Vinci is often referred to as a "T-shaped" individual due to his wide range of talents and expertise. Beyond being a masterful painter, he delved into engineering, music, geology, astronomy, and literature, showcasing a breadth and depth of knowledge that epitomizes the concept of a polymath. While the term "polymath" accurately describes da Vinci's multifaceted abilities, in the modern world we might also describe him as a "versatilist."

A versatilist is not dissimilar to a polymath, although the subtle difference is that the versatilist is one who is masterful at adapting themselves to new areas of inquiry. Their core skill is, essentially, to transfer their skills to whatever new challenge they find themselves in.

This adaptability is crucial in a rapidly changing world, making versatilists highly sought after by organizations grappling with change management. Today, there is more and more interest in these meta-skills, and the value of "apex imaginators," thought leaders and trend-breakers, is becoming apparent as resources become scarce and global complexity skyrockets.

Enter the concept of the "T-shaped person." This is someone whose skill and knowledge sets have a highly developed niche skill, but also a broad and comparatively shallow knowledge base from which this deeper skill emerges. In the letter T, the vertical bar represents depth in a particular field, and the horizontal bar symbolizes the ability to draw insights widely from interdisciplinary areas. It's a particularly effective blend of **breadth versus depth**.

In today's professional landscape, we are now told that individuals with a "T" shaped skill set, combining specialization and versatility, are highly valued for their capacity to contribute effectively across diverse domains and problem-solving scenarios. The two opposing tendencies complement and mitigate one another. The breadth understanding helps anchor and contextualize the depth understanding, while the depth understanding centers and gives meaning to the breadth. Thus, a T-shaped person will never be a superficial generalist, but they'll also avoid becoming mired in obscurity, learning evermore about a teeny-tiny niche that they nevertheless fail to connect to anything else.

T-Shaped Person

An "I-shaped person" is the one who possesses depth knowledge—which is not a bad thing, and a natural place for many of us to start. You may leave college or other specialist training as an I-shaped person because your sole focus has been on deeply understanding a small area of knowledge and developing a skill set far beyond the level required of a layperson.

On the other hand, a "dash-shaped person" lacks any of this specialist knowledge, knowing a little about a lot of different things and applying themselves happily to most areas, although only ever as an amateur. This is also not a bad place to start, especially if you're entering a field as a new hobbyist or simply for interest.

While the I-shaped person is a potentially out-of-touch expert, and the dash-shaped person is a "jack of all trades but master of none," the T-shaped person is a "jack of all trades but master of at least one," i.e., the best of both worlds.

Conceivably there is a pi-shaped person (π) who possesses not one but two areas of depth expertise, but this may be an extremely rare achievement, especially today.

Even if your goals are not professional ones, becoming a T-shaped person has a host of benefits. You learn to collaborate better with other people simply because you're able to communicate and share ideas with those of all different interests and backgrounds. Having both depth and breadth interests means you can switch focus from time to time, maintaining your interest. You're like a knowledge whale—able to dive deep and explore the depths, but also knowing when to come up for air when necessary and scan the horizon.

Your creativity will improve, but so will your appreciation of other people's depth work. You'll be better able to discern any and all information that comes your way because you have developed an understanding of what it takes to achieve that sort of depth in one's chosen field. You become a more interesting person, no doubt, but you also become a more interested person, having charted the edges of both the outer and the lower depths.

How to Cultivate Both Depth and Breadth
Assess Your Current Skills and Base Knowledge

First, make an honest appraisal of your skill set as it stands. Create a self-assessment spreadsheet listing all skills and knowledge. Now, obviously this is going to be a very approximate estimation, but you may be surprised at just what you find when you stop to tally everything up. Sometimes the distinction between skill and knowledge is fuzzy; sometimes it isn't. Use your own discretion to measure appropriately in your chosen area.

You can (and ideally should) conduct this rating procedure in the way that best makes sense to you and the goals and values you've identified for yourself. One possibility is to rate each area on a scale of 0 to 5 to determine your proficiency, where 0 is novice and 5 is expert, as follows:

0—*Stone cold beginner level.* You know basically nothing about this topic and have zero practice with any of the related skills. All you may have is a knowledge that this area exists at all, and a desire and curiosity to know more.

1—*Novice level.* You're on the path to learning, but you still know very little. This is akin to beginning to read relevant publications and articles, "idiot's guide" level texts, and something akin to the first semester of a first-year college-level course.

2—*Advanced to moderate beginner level.* At this level you are able to perform the skill to some degree and have grasped the basics, but you still rely on a mentor and need to check your work constantly.

3—*Competency level.* This is the level at which you're essentially able to take the training wheels off and perform adequately on your own. You're no longer a beginner, but you're not a professional either. You can apply what you've learned, but there's still a lot to learn.

4—*Proficiency level.* This is the realm where you start to perform at far higher than the average. You can do what most people can't. You're not a master, but you're excellent and know your topic inside and out.

5—*Expert level.* This may be hard to describe, but truly mastering something is a little like having brought it completely into your DNA— you can do the thing automatically, effortlessly, almost on intuition. At this level you may contribute and change the field, and your contributions may expand and deepen existing knowledge. You can also teach, and well.

Depending on your subject area, you may wish to have more or fewer levels, but don't get too hung up on the details. Next, carefully note the skills you want to improve and maintain. What needs work and what is well-achieved so far? Where are you comfortable and where do you want to push yourself to do more? Feel free to add a new skill that you want to learn, too, but don't overwhelm yourself. At the same time, don't take what you know and can do for granted—you are probably more skilled than you think!

Start Shaping Your T

As you appraise each skill and knowledge set, decide on where you want your future efforts to focus on. Thinking about each area of skill and knowledge development, go through each of these considerations:

1. **Improvement**
   Make a note of what skills or subskills could use some work. For example, you may be a singer who realizes you'd like to work more on your overall confidence levels, as well as your vibrato and head voice. This is the area of potential depth.
2. **Maintenance**
   What are you happy with currently, no matter its level? It's not possible or desirable to keep learning forever in every single area. You may be a chef who decides you're comfortable with your current pastry skills and don't really need or wish to expand on that for the time being. What will be required, though, is ongoing maintenance. Bear in mind that in many fields, things change quickly, so staying still is the same as

going backward. You may need to keep on learning a little anyway just to stay current. These areas form the top part of your T.

3. **Addition**

   Identify those things you score around 0 or 1 on but want to learn more about. This is like extending the size of the top portion of your T. This is necessary if you're currently an I-shaped person and want to diversify, but is less appropriate if you're already over-burdened with too many separate interests. For example, if you're a marketer who is proficient at social media campaigns, but you know nothing about video creation, photography, copywriting, or AdWords, you may wish to start learning a little more. It's up to you to decide whether these new areas remain *breadth* topics or become *depth* topics over time.

4. **Depth**

   Lastly, take a look at what you currently are an expert at or else wish to be an expert at. You may have no "tail" on your T at all, or you may wish to extend the one you have. This is the single area that you will be focusing most of your attention, time, and energy on, so it's worth prioritizing carefully.

You Decide Your Personal Curriculum

Even if you are in a highly structured training program or are following the guidance of a mentor or tutor, it is still your responsibility to oversee your overall life curriculum. A mentor or lecturer can tell you how best to approach a certain task, but they can't tell you whether you should attempt it in the first place, or what it should mean to you.

Renaissance thinkers like da Vinci were almost exclusively self-directed learners. They certainly took inspiration from conventions around them, but they invariably took it upon themselves to navigate their own learning path, decide their own goals, and set their own learning standards to reach those goals. Being a lifelong learner also requires that we are lifelong teachers—of ourselves. Deliberately considering the shape of our expertise, as we have done in this chapter, means not allowing ourselves to passively fall into default habits about what to focus on and to what extent. Here are a few principles to bear in mind when designing your own curriculum.

Develop Consistent Habits

Establishing habits is crucial for T-shaped development, whether that's for maintenance or improvement. To integrate new skills and activities into your routine, add it to your daily to-do list and cultivate self-discipline to keep it there until it becomes more or less automatic. You can use various tools and apps to help you ensure consistency, especially if you're prone to procrastination, but they're not strictly necessary.

At the same time, engage in practical projects related to your chosen skills, providing real-world application and reinforcing continuous learning. For instance, if you're learning WordPress, create a personal website or explore freelance opportunities to enhance your practical proficiency. Chip away at it every day until this kind of work becomes second nature. Consistency is key.

Evaluate Progress Systematically

Regularly assessing your progress is essential for effective development—otherwise, you won't really know if your efforts are being wasted, or if there is something you need to adjust.

There are many ways to do this; pick one and stick to it. You can read a recent paper in your field of study and rate your understanding on a scale of 1 to 5. Keep that paper and return to it a few months later—what's changed?

Take a piece of paper and articulate everything you know about a specific topic—make a "brain dump" without consulting any outside sources. Then, identify knowledge gaps and areas for improvement. Zoom in on the things you're not clear about or don't understand well. Once you've spent some time on it, do the exercise again and compare your notes—what else is missing?

Share your skills with someone else, providing immediate feedback. This process of teaching someone what we know, akin to the Feynman technique, reveals areas of weakness. If learning a new language, record yourself discussing a random topic for five minutes. Analyze your performance, then repeat once a month. Not only will you monitor your progress, but you'll also give yourself a boost of confidence when you see how far you've come.

Don't Be Afraid to Dabble

Culturally, many of us have been taught not to be "quitters" and believe that if we embark on some skill area, we need to immediately be the very best at it that we can. Give yourself permission to ignore this convention and dabble! You don't have to monetize every skill you have, you don't have to compete, and you don't have to immediately make every whim and fancy your new calling in life. Just be interested.

Don't Let Other People Tell You What You Find Important

Perhaps you think that you "should" learn to code, or that you "should" learn something about cryptocurrencies or take up weightlifting or meditation or beekeeping or whatever. There are fads and fashions in all things, but try to avoid letting them dictate where you put *your* precious and finite attention. Only you can say what your values are, and what fires you up. If you genuinely don't find something interesting or useful, feel free to ignore it. Even the great da Vinci couldn't do everything, and he didn't attempt it.

Prioritize, But Stay Switched On

T-shaped people spend most of their lives on the main stem of their T. Even though they have diverse interests and understandings, they know what it means to prioritize. When time is short or resources limited, they will choose to focus on their main skill every single time. Da Vinci woke up and he was, first and foremost, a painter. That said, such versatilists do pop up from out of their depths occasionally to take in whatever new opportunities, emerging issues, or other changes are afoot, so they can stay alert to evolving possibilities.

Mix Hard and Soft Skills

Finally, try to keep a varied mix of different skills and interests. Offset certain serious and abstract skills with more physically demanding or practical ones. While you improve your general intelligence, don't forget to work on your social skills, character, and moral development. A comprehensive curriculum will challenge you to develop yourself to the full potential of all your capacities as a human being, not just the commercial or academic ones.

Connecting the Unconnected

"All knowledge is connected to all other knowledge. The fun is in making the connections."

Arthur Aufderheide

Da Vinci's concept of "connecting the unconnected" refers to the deliberate linking of seemingly unrelated ideas, concepts, or observations to stimulate creativity and generate innovative insights. This approach is reflected in his practice of exploring connections between disparate subjects, often through imaginative and unconventional means.

Leonardo da Vinci's creative process, as evident from his notebooks, involved a strategic approach to art and invention. Instead of creating idealized or preconceived images, he applied a systematic method of combining the best elements from various observations to achieve a unique and captivating result. This technique is exemplified in his most famous works, such as the *Mona Lisa* and *The Last Supper*.

In the case of the *Mona Lisa*, da Vinci is believed to have assembled the features of many beautiful faces rather than attempting to depict a singular, conventionally beautiful one. The painting's allure and the perceived variety of expressions on the subject's face could be attributed to da Vinci's purposeful combination of the most appealing features he had observed. This approach adds a layer of complexity and mystery to the painting, as viewers interpret and discover different expressions within the amalgamation of features.

Likewise, in his composition of *The Last Supper*, da Vinci didn't merely reproduce a common scene of Jesus Christ with the twelve apostles. Instead, he applied a combinatorial approach, possibly creating a matrix of elements, such as apostles, types of reactions, conditions, facial expressions, and situations. Through experimentation with variations and combinations of these elements, da Vinci breathed new life and meaning into the scene, surpassing the efforts of his predecessors. The result was a masterpiece that conveyed a depth and significance that set it apart from other renditions of the same subject.

To grasp the power of potential connections, consider the following basic example. First think of the pairing of a rabbit with a cat. When these two things are put together, what do you perceive overall? Your mind may look for similarities—for example, the fact that they're both smallish, furry mammals. But if we now connect the rabbit with something else, say a carrot, then what does the picture look like? A new relationship is suggested, and we think about the rabbit eating the carrot, perhaps.

Understanding the rabbit, the cat, or the carrot in isolation is one task in itself, but when we consider these phenomena as connected to other phenomena, suddenly the way we see them changes. By connecting certain ideas to other ideas, we literally change the way our brain is able to perceive and think about them. This opens up vast new possibilities for creativity and problem solving. By paying attention to context, to pattern, and to the way we make metaphors, we can actively use this power of connection to draw out and emphasize new and unexpected aspects hidden in the most ordinary things.

Da Vinci suggested that the world was teeming with new ideas if you would only look and allow your brain to find new patterns and links. He advised people to look at the ashes of a fire, the shape of clouds, or even just marks on a wall to discover pleasing new shapes and images. In the trees and landscapes around him, he saw the beginnings of human movement that would eventually find its way onto canvas or paper.

It's even been suggested that da Vinci would sometimes throw a paint-soaked sponge at a wall and spend time examining the random shapes it made. He did this once when puzzling over his newest fascination—ways to transport people—and in the paint splodges he thought he saw a man riding a horse, only instead of a horse's legs there were wheels. What if you could combine a horse with wheels? Thus, da Vinci invented the bicycle (actually, this myth has subsequently been debunked, but the example is still a good one!).

How to Use da Vinci's Attribute Technique

Let's try to find a systematic rather than intuitive way to start making fruitful connections.

Da Vinci's method involved analyzing the structure of a subject, breaking down its major parameters (main categories), and listing attributes (variations) for each parameter. He then generated new and innovative ideas by systematically combining these variations into different configurations. It's a process you can repeat no matter what your chosen field of learning. Here's how.

Step 1. Identify the problem and its parameters. What problem are you trying to solve, or at the very least, what area are you investigating, and to what end?

Step 2. Break down the problem into its constituent parameters. The parameters are the basic framework or guidelines underpinning the problem. How many you include is up to you, but keep it manageable. One way to identify truly instrumental parameters is to ask whether your current problem or situation would persist without the parameter in question.

Step 3. You can visualize each parameter as a column on a table. Now, for each row on the table, you want to list as many attributes as you can under each parameter. An attribute here can be understood as a variation or option. Again, you can have as many attributes as you like, and the more you generate, the greater your chance of uncovering some as-yet-unseen connection that proves illuminating. A table of just ten parameters, with ten attributes/variations each, will yield *ten billion combinations*.

Step 4. Once you've set up your table, you can now pick randomly through it as though it were a "random connection generator." Select one attribute from each column and combine it with another randomly chosen attribute from the next column, and so on until you've covered all the parameters. Don't be in too much of a hurry to look for something meaningful. Just brainstorm and keep comparing the links you generate with Step 1—your problem/situation as you understand it. It may be that you end up recreating the table after you realize that certain attributes and parameters are more fruitful, or you may return to Step 1 to redefine the problem. The process is iterative.

Now, that's all very abstract—let's take a look at an example to illustrate the concept. Let's imagine that the owner of a small bakery and farm shop is trying to expand their business. They're trying to think of new products or services to offer their clientele, but they're stumped, so they try da Vinci's process as outlined above. Step 1 was pretty simple: The goal was to identify some new market, product, or activity that could make the business more money.

The owner then draws up a table that looks like the one below. Along the top, they label the columns to indicate different parameters (products sold, customer type), and under each of these headings they list a potential variation. They don't overanalyze, but just brainstorm and put things down.

Products sold	Customer type	Mode of selling	Presentation of products	Seasonal/periodic
Farm produce	Retired people	Standard supermarket layout	Rustic, packageless	Christmas
Freshly baked goods	Families	"Click and collect"	Bulk	Sunday market
Frozen	Young	Order online	Artful	Morning cafe

goods to bake at home	adults			
Supermarket brands	"Foodies"	Catalogue	Eco-friendly	School holidays
Novelties	Other industries	Subscription service	Foreign/exotic	Valentine's Day

So far, this is just a framework of possibilities (and much shortened here—the real exercise will produce a larger and more detailed table). The owner now runs through some random combinations, for example:

- Novelties + "foodies" + Catalogue + eco-friendly + Christmas
- Frozen goods + retired people + subscription service + bulk + Valentine's Day
- Farm produce + families + standard supermarket layout + foreign/exotic + school holidays
- Etc.

As you can see, some interesting ideas are already starting to emerge. The owner thinks about marketing a line of order-in-bulk ready meals for pensioners who are not interested in cooking, and starts to brainstorm fresh ideas in this area (perhaps with a new table). Or they may decide to start issuing a free catalogue advertising some exclusive imported Christmas foods to appeal to gourmands and connoisseurs every year.

Naturally, most of the options generated by this table will not be viable, but that's beside the point. By throwing random things together, you're giving yourself the chance to look at all these elements with fresh eyes and start building on the seeds of what could grow into great ideas later on. Don't be too quick to dismiss an idea if it seems like a bizarre connection—what if they did fit together? *How* could they fit together?

Similarly, think of ways that you can continuously expand your parameters or play with their attributes. You may think you've listed all the possible yearly holidays under the "seasonal" parameter, but what about the holidays that various immigrant groups may celebrate in your area? Is anyone catering to *them*, and if not, could this be an untapped market? This is a possibility you might not have considered before literally seeing the "exotic/foreign" attribute right next to the "seasonal" one.

The Language of Metaphor

Another way to practice the deliberate art of connecting the unconnected is to liberally use metaphor. Metaphors are so deeply woven into the way we think and communicate that often they're invisible to us. A good metaphor, however, not only helps us grasp a more complex or abstract idea, but it also helps us *generate* those ideas.

Think, for example, about da Vinci's supposed encounter with the splotches on the wall that looked like a horse, but only with wheels. This is in fact a metaphor: A bicycle is *like* a horse, but with wheels. The metaphor highlights the core attribute of both things being compared: their use as modes of transport. By connecting these two things, you can both imagine and communicate a very particular idea—that there is potential variation in this parameter. Not only would the metaphor help da Vinci explain what a bicycle was to someone who may have never seen one before (but had seen a horse), he could also use the metaphor itself to generate further metaphors, ideas, and possibilities. For example, if a bicycle is like a horse, then what kind of contraption is like a fish? Or a crocodile? Is there a machine that's like a human in the way that a bicycle is like a horse? Meta-metaphors!

Think of metaphor (and simile for that matter) as a complete language in itself. This is a paradoxical language because the rule is that we can understand a thing more clearly by describing *other* things. Using metaphor, we can condense complicated ideas into more manageable ones—thus allowing ourselves to comprehend and remember more. Metaphor also allows us to "bootstrap" learning by connecting something new and unknowable to something we already know and understand. For example, take a look at these metaphors:

- In logic and philosophy: A good argument is like a tabletop, and the premises are like its legs. The table "stands" level and sound when the premises are sufficient and well-ordered underneath it.
- In biology: The pattern of predation in an ecosystem is a "food chain"—each animal is like a link in that chain.
- In physics: The atom is like a mini planet, with electrons orbiting around it like tiny moons.

In fact, being proficient at metaphorical thinking allows you to more clearly understand the existence and role of theory itself. Good metaphors are so effective at helping us understand things that they often become part of how we think of that concept. For example, the idea of an "ecosystem" is merely a mathematical and theoretical model that represents a reality that is too complex to be charted this way. Many people are surprised to learn, however, that ecological models have significant limitations and bear as much relation to the real world as a two-dimensional map bears to an actual landscape.

When you understand what narratives, concepts, models, ideologies, and consensus metaphors are currently being used in any field, you are able to start looking more closely at them: Could another, more illuminating metaphor be found? Indeed, many major scientific revolutions often come with a paradigm-shifting switch to a new metaphor. For example, during the Victorian era, when machinery was steam powered and portions of the world were still undiscovered, people spoke of the human mind in terms of territories charted and uncharted; Freud's "hydraulic" conception of the mind was an elaborate metaphor that came directly from the culture he inhabited.

Today, our metaphors of the human mind are different—we liken them to computers, imagining our memories have been stored and filed away as though in a hard drive, and visualizing the neural connections as electrical circuits or nodes on a motherboard. But consider: what new things about the brain might you discover if you used a completely different metaphor? Could the mind also be a forest, or a kind of organism, a spaceship, a fancy dress costume, a cathedral, a cloud?

Summary:

- Leonardo Da Vinci is often referred to as a "T-shaped" individual due to his wide range of talents and expertise paired with impressive depth in some areas; today he'd be called a versatilist. To become more of a T-shaped person yourself, first assess your current skills and base knowledge to determine where skill and knowledge are lacking. Honestly appraise your current skill level and identify which areas need improvement, maintenance, addition, or work to increase depth.
- Then, even if you are already in a structured training program, devise your own curriculum and be disciplined in following your own learning goals according to what you discover in the above exercise—don't simply default to other people's values and principles. Set consistent habits to work on

your goal daily and have a means to monitor your progress.
- Keep a balance of hard and soft skills. Know what your priorities are, but don't be afraid to dabble now and then just out of curiosity.
- One of the polymath's greatest skills is the ability to connect the unconnected. You can use da Vinci's attribute technique to systematically uncover fresh ideas and combinations. Break the problems down into a series of parameters and then brainstorm as many variations/attributes as possible for each that you can. Run through the table of possibilities without preconceptions or judgment to uncover new possibilities.
- In a similar way, get comfortable with the language of metaphor, which not only helps us to grasp more complex or abstract ideas, but it also helps us generate those ideas.

Chapter 4: Get Organized

Da Vincian Note-Taking

"Great things are done by a series of small things brought together."

Vincent van Gogh

It's arguable that mankind invented language to serve as a kind of external brain—by putting our ideas out there in the world and recording them in pen and ink, we were able to relieve the burden on our memories, gain a little psychological distance from our ideas, and communicate our concepts far more widely than any oral society ever could. Writing was not evidence of our learning—it was *how* we learned.

Writing and reading are tools for expanding the capacities of the mind, but what this means is that if you want to learn something, you'll probably end up generating enormous amounts of notes, papers, books, and other miscellany! To keep your growing "second brain" in good enough order that it serves you well, you'll need to be organized.

Visit any exhibition of da Vinci's work and you might be struck by just how beautiful—and meticulous—his notes were. The man was a doodler and could positively fill a page with diagrams, illustrations, and text, written both backward and forward. Any note-taking method is a good one if it works for your goals, but you could try experimenting with an approach inspired by da Vinci to create notes that are more visually rich and interesting, and which are most conducive to creativity and those all-important connections already discussed.

Da Vinci's approach may appeal to those who find the usual advice for note-taking doesn't work for them. You don't need any fancy apps or tools—you don't need to spend money at all. A simple notebook and writing implement are enough. The technique is simple: Divide every page into two, left- and right-hand sides. On the right is where you put down your observations, various facts and details, thoughts, and so on, and on the left, you put your own thoughts and feelings about what's on the right. Here you include the same information but paraphrased in your own words, or even sketched and diagrammed out to help you better understand it. The left column is where you process what's on the left, be that with a sketch, a question, a link to some other idea or text, or even a refutation.

Theoretical physicist Richard Feynman taught the world the power of explaining a concept in your own words and without invoking any further technical jargon. This way, you could determine whether you truly did grasp the fundamentals of the concept rather than simply know how to regurgitate the right words for it. Da Vinci practiced Feynman's technique before there was a Feynman and had no trouble "translating" everything he encountered into his own vivid, multimedia imagination.

Actively make connections between disparate ideas, identify patterns and relationships among different pieces of information, and engage with what you read to make it your own. Producing these two-sided notes is also a great way to record rich information that will be far better memorized, and the page will always be personalized to your learning style. In fact, if you keep returning to your notes and adding to them as you learn, the notes become both a learning resource and a record of your learning journey. You can use them to track and monitor your progress, or else return to them during exam preparation.

Other things you might like to include on your page:

- Use headings and subheadings to help create levels and hierarchy.
- Add your own doodles, diagrams, or drawings.
- Scribble your immediate response or even a question you have.
- Emphasize a few keywords that stand out to you.
- Make mini mind maps (or not so mini ones!).

- Literally draw links to other concepts and ideas—even if they span pages. You can denote the kind of connection by changing the style of the line linking them. For example, a dashed line for a weak or possible connection, but a bold, triple line for a very strong or important one (maybe a jagged line for an adversarial relationship? Arrows to show directionality?).
- Make mini, easy-to-understand summaries of more complex or lengthy processes. See if you can boil things down to a single sentence, image, or symbol.
- Convert the data you see on the right into another form—for example, a graph or chart.
- Have a "conversation" with the material and argue back or write down your initial reaction.
- Quickly note down any spontaneous or creative ideas that come to you when reading what's on the left. Don't be afraid to use humor, either!
- Make a note of what else this idea connects to or *could* connect to. Does it undermine or contradict anything that went before?
- Use symbols and shorthand of your own design—little annotations that will help you understand the complexity of an idea at a glance.
- . . . and whatever else you can invent!

Whatever your notes ultimately end up looking like, try to remember that they are there to serve you, not the other way around. Your goal should never be to create some impressive-looking notes that rival the beauty of da Vinci's, but rather to begin constructing that second brain that will make your *thought processes* beautiful. If, for example, drawings and doodles don't work for you, don't try to force them in somehow. If you discover you want to include a third column for some reason, go ahead and try it.

Your notes are a place where you work—you experiment with new concepts, break things down, build them up again, keeps record of things you don't want to forget, and leave a little mental breadcrumb trail to help you find your way back after a possibly windy trip into the metaphorical forest! Throughout, your notes should be working hard for you, helping you analyze, summarize, contextualize, and engage. It can get messy!

Here are a few further ideas to help you organize your note-taking—although, again, try not to copy something you see someone else doing just because it looks smart. The best note system is the one that works best for *you* and what you're trying to learn.

Include a Summary Section at the End of Each Page

It can be quite useful to have a section at the bottom (or top) of every page where you briefly summarize its contents. As you compile the notes, this practice serves as a reminder to continually pause and absorb what you've learned. It's like a checkpoint where you bank what you've learned before taking in the next section. The mini summary also gives you a chance to paraphrase in your own words as well as see at a glance what each page refers to, making it easier to handle for future reference.

Instead of Notebooks, Consider Files

A notebook is itself a kind of metaphor—it strongly suggests a linear pattern of organization! But if you're frequently adding, removing, or changing up the order of your study material, you may wish instead to have free sheets of paper that you then move around as necessary. Have one central file and then as many smaller files as you need for each subcategory. Liberally use color-coded markers, file dividers, sticky tabs, little decals, and highlighters to annotate your work. You could use a file punch to include material from elsewhere, dog ear a page, or even cut and paste in pieces of other notebooks, prints, lists, doodles, and random ephemera.

Regularly Prune Back Your Notes

Not every thought is a great one, and not every idea needs to be pursued. Many of the notes you produce will be more along the lines of clutter than precious records. That's okay—just get rid of them. While it may seem like a chore, regularly going through your notes is a way to revise and consolidate what you've learned (and still need to learn), but it's also a way to refine your records and trim away anything that has now become irrelevant. Can you take three similar documents and combine them into a single, more attractive one? The process is not just aesthetic—you may be surprised how much fresh insight you can derive just by rearranging old material you thought you were already familiar with.

Don't Forget to Bring Something with You . . .

Inspiration can strike at the most random times (in fact, that's almost exclusively the times it tends to strike!), so you'd better be prepared. Have a smaller, traveling notebook to keep on you at all times, and a little pen or pencil. You may like to just use a note-taking app on your phone, but there is something extremely satisfying about the tactile act of scribbling on paper—and it's often quicker to do. Jot down any random thoughts, ideas that come to you, things you overhear, or random connections you stumble on and don't want to forget.

Let Your Notes Be "Fluid"

As we saw with da Vinci's attribute technique, there is hidden magic waiting in unexpected combinations, if only we stop to shuffle things around so we can uncover them. There is also a less deliberate way in which we can support our mind's ability to connect the unconnected, and that's with the way we keep notes and make records. The connections may be subtle and somewhat hidden, but they're there. For example, da Vinci was always fascinated with the science of optics and wrote about his observations on the nature of the eye and of light. He developed his own *sfumato* technique that couldn't help but be inspired by this understanding and come through in his paintings, which were known for being lifelike and full of character. The *Mona Lisa*, too, owes much of her charm and mystery to the fact that da Vinci was at the time intrigued by anatomy— her famous smile might not have been what it is today without da Vinci's background research into the function of the tiny muscles around the mouth and cheeks.

In similar ways, all of da Vinci's innovations and insights were informed by the totality of his learning; the fullness of the Renaissance man was always reflected in his works one way or another. You can follow suit by not making artificial barriers between separate subjects— the great thinking of the past didn't. If you learn something interesting at the gym that can be applied to your work with coding or math or flower arranging, then make sure your notes are able to help you record that observation. "Fluid" notes will allow material to easily cross-pollinate from one area of inquiry to another.

A To-Do List Is Also a To-Learn List

"The best thing for being sad," replied Merlin, beginning to puff and blow, "is to learn something. That's the only thing that never fails. You may grow old and trembling in your anatomies, you may lie awake at night listening to the disorder of your veins, you may miss your only love, you may see the world about you devastated by evil lunatics, or know your honour trampled in the sewers of baser minds. There is only one thing for it then—to learn. Learn why the world wags and what wags it. That is the only thing which the mind can never exhaust, never alienate, never be tortured by, never fear or distrust, and never dream of regretting. Learning is the only thing for you. Look what a lot of things there are to learn."

T.H. White, The Once and Future King

Leonardo da Vinci, a true polymath and pioneer in cross-disciplinary thought, would easily fit into today's society with his diverse skills and interests—and if he couldn't find a role for himself, he'd likely invent one! Beyond being an extraordinary painter, creating masterpieces like *The Last Supper* and the *Mona Lisa*, he delved into physics, studying anatomy, fluids, and light. His talent, still recognized and admired today, was not any of these particular skills, but his ability to learn more generally.

Da Vinci's extensive collection of notebooks provides a unique glimpse into his mind and reveals that, just like us mortal moderns, he kept to-do lists. But here, we see evidence of a different mind at work. His lists, captured in handwritten notes, showcase not only the convergence of his diverse interests, but his overall approach to learning. Unlike the typical notion of organization, da Vinci's notes started in a divergent manner, reflecting a mind fascinated by *everything*. Each list looks a little like a snapshot of his mind: It was busy in there! The digitized version of his notebook by the British Museum reveals the juxtaposition of seemingly unrelated elements, such as a cockle shell alongside notes on weights and balance.

Compared to today's conventional to-do list philosophy, da Vinci's technique was very different. Thinking now about your own list of tasks, how do you feel about it? If you're like most people, a to-do list is a horrible thing and looks more or less like this:

- Thing you hate but have to do
- Another thing you hate
- Weird email???
- That thing you procrastinated doing yesterday
- Some kind of impossible thing here
- Buy dishwasher tabs
- Boring thing

- One more thing you hate and just know you won't have time for
- A thing you haven't done for weeks and makes you feel increasingly guilty and resentful
- Work out
- Etc.

Look familiar?

If you can find it in you to do all these things, then your reward is another list, almost identical, to complete the next day. In other words, most of us probably view to-do lists as a boring, stressful grind. It's also about what we *have to* do.

For da Vinci, the feeling of his lists was totally different. It was about what he *wanted* to do. His to-do list was more like a to-learn list, and you can almost feel the curiosity radiating from some of the pages we've managed to preserve from da Vinci's time.

Leonardo da Vinci's notebook, as noted by historian Toby Lester, reveals a remarkable to-do list that highlights the artist's extraordinary motivation and drive—not his commitment to drudgery. The list, from the early 1490s, was translated by Robert Krulwich of NPR and showcases da Vinci's dedication to learning and creating, even when faced with seemingly impossible tasks. The items on the list provide a glimpse into the ambitious goals and diverse interests that fueled da Vinci's prolific mind during that period:

Here's an example of da Vinci's to-do list provided by Krulwich:

1. *[Calculate] the measurement of Milan and suburbs*
2. *[Find] a book that treats of Milan and its churches, which is to be had at the stationer's on the way to Cordusio*
3. *Get the master of arithmetic to show you how to square a triangle*
4. *Get Messea Fazio (a professor of medicine and law in Pavia) to show you about proportion*
5. *Examine the crossbow of Maestro Gianetto*
6. *Ask Benedetto Portinari (a Florentine merchant) by what means they go on ice in Flanders*
7. *[Ask about] the measurement of the sun promised me by Maestro Giovanni Francese*

As you can see, Leonardo didn't just write down things he needed to do. He created an ambitious list of all those nooks and crannies in his world that he was burningly curious about and wanted to learn more.

Under industrialized consumer capitalism, curiosity is not directly profitable, and therefore it's discouraged. What is encouraged is measurable, concrete outputs that generate money, and preferably as fast as possible. Working in these conditions, it's not surprising that our to-do lists start to look like slave drivers, not to mention our own curiosity and even joy at learning and discovering is seen as a distraction, a threat, or even a kind of unearned indulgence.

There's probably a lot more to say about the ideology of the to-do list, but suffice to say that it doesn't *have to* be that way. We don't *have to* divide our lives into work versus play, legitimate versus illegitimate, productive versus unproductive. Inspired by the great inventor and creator da Vinci, we can make our first task the invention of our own system.

When you were a child, you were naturally curious about everything and asked nine million questions a day (slight exaggeration). As an adult you have been taught to set all that aside unless your curiosity can be productively channeled into an existing and approved path. So, you have your dedicated work hours, and if you should become curious or fascinated by something during that time, you call it disciplined to forcefully ignore that impulse and instead bring your attention back to things that matter: the things on the to-do list. If you fail to do this, you call it daydreaming or distraction, or else diagnose yourself with a procrastination problem—the solution for which is more to-do lists!

What if you considered following this curiosity as the "real work" of life and recategorized the drudgery as the distraction?

What if you prioritized your natural and spontaneous inquiry into the world around you and found a way to sort out the dishwasher tabs and emails afterward, once the more important stuff has been done?

Now, nobody is suggesting that you run off and follow every whim that occurs to you while neglecting your real-world duties and obligations. A person who doesn't pay the bills or remember to buy groceries is not going to be able to probe the mysteries of the universe for very long! Nevertheless, it can be worthwhile to begin cultivating a mindset shift and purposefully giving curiosity, passion, and interest a more central place in your life.

Every single time you find curiosity and interest welling up in you, seize it with both hands. Write it down somewhere. Put your questions in a notebook and allow them to marinate for a while. Then, when you have the time and energy, consult this list and deliberately chip away at it. Convert those questions into tasks that will systematically help you find answers. If you haven't written any of this down, there's a strong chance a flash of insight will strike, and by the time you get around to taking a closer look, the impulse has faded, or you've forgotten about it entirely. Imagine how many eureka moments are lost because we're "busy" on social media or watching TV!

Archimedes' "Shower Thought"

Let's take a closer look at the idea of the "eureka moment" because it can tell us a lot about the kind of mindset that generates genuine solutions to problems. Around 200 BC lived a man whom da Vinci himself admired as a great mathematician, astronomer, and physicist—the famed Archimedes, still considered one of the greatest scientists of all time.

The following tale took place almost 2,300 years ago, and yet it still contains fresh wisdom for us today. The story goes that Sicilian King Hieron II of Syracuse gave a goldsmith a bar of gold and instructed him to fashion it into a crown. The goldsmith did so, but the crown the king received made him suspicious, and he wondered whether he had mixed in some cheaper metal, like silver, and kept some of the gold for himself. The king couldn't prove anything, however, and so consulted Archimedes to help him solve the puzzle. Archimedes happily accepted the challenge and asked for a few days to ponder over it.

A little while later Archimedes was taking a bath, and he noticed that it was so full of water that when he stepped in, some water splashed out and onto the floor. Getting even further in made more water splash out. Supposedly he had a flash of insight into the problem of the king's crown that was so exciting, he immediately raced around naked, shouting, "Eureka!" or, "I have found it!"

The astonishing insight was this: When he climbed into the bath, his body displaced some water, and when he climbed further, more water was displaced. He concluded that there was a direct relationship between his volume and the volume of the water, reasoning that if he had been smaller, less water would have been displaced. He couldn't help but ask the question, "What if I put the king's crown in water? Would the water it displaced tell me anything about its volume?"

This got him thinking about the crown's density.

Archimedes was aware that gold was denser than silver. So, he took a nugget of gold and a nugget of silver with the same mass and dropped each in turn into a brim-full bowl of water, measuring how much water was displaced over the rim. Can you predict what he found?

Both the gold and silver had the same mass, but silver has a larger volume because it is less dense. If the silver has a larger volume, that means it would displace more water than the same mass of gold. This in turn meant that if the goldsmith had indeed mixed some silver into the crown, then the crown would have a larger volume than a crown made of pure gold. A crown with silver mixed in, therefore, would displace more water even though it weighed the same as a pure gold crown.

Time for an experiment! Archimedes immersed the king's crown in water and immersed a solid gold bar of the same mass in water, too. Then he compared the volume of water that each displaced. Unfortunately for the goldsmith, Archimedes discovered that the king's crown did in fact displace more water—it was not pure gold!

The goldsmith's almost certain execution notwithstanding, this experiment was so successful that Archimedes wrote about it in his book *On Floating Bodies*. Galileo reproduced the experiments and concluded: "to those who have read and understood the very subtle inventions of this divine man in his own writings; from which one most clearly realizes how inferior all other minds are to Archimedes' . . ."

Today, physicists still refer to Archimedes' principle, which says that when a body is immersed in liquid, it is subject to an upward force of buoyancy that equals the weight of the liquid displaced by that body. The principles Archimedes uncovered were used by scientists of all kinds to understand how and why some things float.

Da Vinci admired Archimedes and was not only impressed with the above story, but took inspiration from other works in statics, engineering, firearms, especially those covered in Archimedes' *On Plane Equilibria*. Da Vinci also referred directly to Archimedes on the cover of his own Manuscript F ("*Archimedes, de centro gravitatis*").

Now, this rather long detour into the story of Archimedes is to illustrate that great ideas don't exclusively come from, well, "work." Imagine if Archimedes had the discipline to chain himself to his work desk until he had figured out a solution to the king's problem. The entire bathtub eureka story as we know it might never have existed. His tale is a version of the modern "shower thought" phenomenon, where great insights strike us when we are decidedly not working and simply standing under running water, letting our minds wander.

The reason people are so often struck by sudden insight in these random situations is probably because it is only during these times when our minds are relaxed and unprogrammed enough to experience the upwelling of genuine curiosity. If we are also working, we do not allow our brain enough opportunity to wander off and discover something new. If we are always busy doing what we *should*, we don't get the chance to explore what we *could*.

Of course, Archimedes had to do a whole lot more than just have a eureka moment—there had to be a series of experiments and a process of reasoning that followed that insight to bring him to the answer he wanted. This shaping of the path of initial curiosity is what a to-learn list is for.

How to Chase Your Own Eureka Moments

Always Carry a Notebook

Great thinkers, artists, inventors, and business moguls throughout history (not just da Vinci but Isaac Newton, Beethoven, Benjamin Franklin, Thomas Edison, John D. Rockefeller, Bill Gates, and even Richard Branson) were all known for carrying pocketbooks. The practice is all about jotting down ideas, details about new acquaintances, interesting things heard, intriguing questions, and more. This allows you to capture your mini-insights and make use of them, rather than have them fly off again and be forgotten.

Embrace Random Thoughts and Doodling

Allowing the mind to "let go" and engage in free-floating thoughts and doodling is considered essential for creative minds. The idea is supported by research showing that individuals with ADHD, known for their spontaneous thinking, daydreaming, and impulsivity, often exhibit high levels of creative thought and achievement. This practice encourages a mindset that goes beyond focused attention, potentially leading to increased creativity. Schedule plenty of "unprogrammed" time to let your mind rest, digest, and process. It can be surprising just how strong the brain's tendency is for generating random new ideas. Just be careful not to allow a "productive" work mindset to creep in and start assigning you tasks!

Turn Curiosity into Action

Archimedes' initial "aha!" moment was followed by a storm of new questions. The only way to answer them was to design follow-up experiments and go out looking for useful data. Your to-learn list will function best when it allows you to convert questions and interesting ideas into real-life action. Look again at da Vinci's list above and notice how many verbs there are—examine, ask, calculate.

This is a subtle reframing of what the to-do list can be—not a series of tasks, but of actions that are all geared toward some specific end. They are not just chores, but instrumental actions that relate directly to your initial curiosity. Da Vinci, for example, once wrote a note to himself in a margin of a notebook to "describe a woodpecker's tongue." Later on, he wrote, "The tongue of a woodpecker can extend more than three times the length of its bill. When not in use, it retracts into the skull and its cartilage-like structure continues past the jaw to wrap around the bird's head and then curve down to its nostril." In New Orleans in 1952, biographer Walter Isaacson wrote a chapter where he playfully sets up an imaginary conversation between the reader, da Vinci, and himself, saying: "There is no reason you actually need to know any of this. But I thought maybe that you would want to know. Just out of curiosity. Pure curiosity."

Summary:

- Getting organized is about bringing "a series of small things together" so that new insight, connection, and understanding can be obtained. Proper note-taking helps you clarify, extend, and deepen your understanding of your work, and acts like a "second brain."
- Your best note-taking system will be one you devise yourself, but experiment with end-of-

page summaries, special notations, questions and comments in the margins, mind maps, and links to other material. Make it fluid and flexible. Use the two-page da Vinci technique to enter into a "dialogue" with your notes that you continually prune and update. Don't forget to bring a small notebook wherever you go!

- A to-do list can be re-imagined as a to-learn list—not based on dull obligation but on interest and curiosity. Mundane chores cannot be avoided, but try to *prioritize* your spontaneous interest and capture fresh ideas when they emerge, taking detailed notes and returning to them later. This may require a deep mindset shift about the divide between work and play and between "should" and "want to." Try to cherish and cultivate your inborn wonder, rather than squashing it in the name of productivity and efficiency.
- Archimedes' eureka moment can teach us a lot about rest, downtime, and obliquely solving problems rather than structured, forceful slogging. We often find insight in the least expected place, when our minds are free to play, explore, and connect randomly.
- Deliberately embrace rest, breaks, unstructured time, and open-ended doodling. Change perspectives and find fresh solutions by regularly stepping back from your work.

Chapter 5: Striking a Balance

Doing and Not Doing

"Sitting quietly, doing nothing, spring comes, and the grass grows by itself."

Zen proverb

Leonardo da Vinci's status as a "Renaissance Man" was characterized by his remarkable talents but also by distractibility and procrastination. Despite his brilliance, many of his projects remained unfinished, including *The Last Supper*, which was completed only after his patron's ultimatum. The iconic *Mona Lisa* took *two decades* to finish, and several other projects, such as the *Adoration of the Magi* and various equestrian endeavors, were never completed at all.

In the *Chronicle for Higher Education*, W.A. Pannapacker writes,

> *"Leonardo rarely completed any of the great projects that he sketched in his notebooks. His groundbreaking research in human anatomy resulted in no publications—at least not in his lifetime. Not only did Leonardo fail to realize his potential as an engineer and a scientist,*

but he also spent his career hounded by creditors to whom he owed paintings and sculptures for which he had accepted payment but—for some reason—could not deliver, even when his deadline was extended by years. His surviving paintings amount to no more than twenty, and five or six, including the Mona Lisa, *were still in his possession when he died. Apparently, he was still tinkering with them. Nowadays, Leonardo might have been hired by a top research university, but it seems likely that he would have been denied tenure. He had lots of notes but relatively little to put in his portfolio."*

Is this description surprising? Many readers may have envisioned da Vinci as a master heavyweight genius, ultra-productive, in command of himself at all times, uber-successful at smashing his goals, and well on his way to being a Renaissance-era celebrity, had such a thing existed then. The picture that emerges from expert biographers, however, is very different: Da Vinci was totally scatterbrained, they tell us. He was an infuriatingly difficult man to pin down, he struggled with money, and he arguably lacked the self-discipline and ruthless ambition of the modern businesspeople who write fawning LinkedIn articles about his genius.

On the other hand, da Vinci's less-celebrated work habits also included drawn-out painting sessions that went from sunrise to sunset, while on other days he'd simply sit motionless, staring at his paintings, and the day would pass without him making a single brushstroke. In fact, the Duke of Milan became so troubled by da Vinci's chaotic work schedule and so worried that it would not be finished, he summoned da Vinci to discuss his concerns.

Da Vinci is said to have defended himself by characterizing his behavior as a kind of productive procrastination—part of the creative process, rather than an impediment to it. He asserted that individuals of great genius often achieve the most when they seem to work the least, as their minds are fearsomely occupied with perfecting ideas and concepts before giving them physical form. The idea was that the finished piece was only the last step in a long, often purely mental process. Though he might not have appeared to be holding a paintbrush or mixing paints, he was in fact painting all the while—just doing the invisible parts!

Pannapacker continues (and it's worth quoting him at length here),

> *"If creative procrastination, selectively applied, prevented Leonardo from finishing a few commissions—of minor importance when one is struggling with the inner workings of the cosmos—then*

> *only someone who is a complete captive of the modern cult of productive mediocrity that pervades the workplace, particularly in academe, could fault him for it.*
>
> *Productive mediocrity requires discipline of an ordinary kind. It is safe and threatens no one. Nothing will be changed by mediocrity; mediocrity is completely predictable . . . Mediocrity is the opposite of what we call "genius." Mediocrity gets perfectly mundane things done on time. But genius is uncontrolled and uncontrollable. You cannot produce a work of genius according to a schedule or an outline. As Leonardo knew, it happens through random insights resulting from unforeseen combinations. Genius is inherently outside the realm of known disciplines and linear career paths."*

Over five centuries later, we are still intrigued by the idea of productive procrastination and the unpredictable and uncontrollable paths that true genius takes. Again, we see how creative genius often breaks down conventional dualistic thinking—in this case, the paradox of working while appearing to be at rest. In our final chapter, we'll be looking more deeply at how we can dissolve the barriers between work and rest, art and science, and even, as shown in da Vinci's trademark mirror writing, left and right! The result is a kind of dynamic equilibrium, a generative balancing act that keeps us in the sweet spot somewhere in between extremes.

Here are a few ideas for exploring the tension between these extremes and finding your own productive balance between them.

Before Diving into a Project, Take the Time to Thoroughly Study and Research the Subject Matter

In 1489, da Vinci was commissioned to design and build a giant bronze horse statue to honor Duke Francesco Sforza. Instead of getting to work at once, however, he spent time on preparation. Lots of time. *Years*, in fact. He studied horse anatomy in depth, sketching and re-sketching different body parts and even dissecting an actual horse when he got the chance. So devoted was he to learning the exact nature of the form of a horse, that one journal from this period contained twenty-nine different measurements of a horse's front leg alone.

After a decade of measurement, observation, and meditation, he finally began the sculpture. Sadly, his work was destroyed by the invading French army, and thus never completed. If it had, we can only imagine the masterpiece it may have been!

Assuming that you probably don't have a decade's worth of wiggle room in your own life (or, for that matter, an invading French army to worry about) you can still take inspiration from da Vinci and *take your time* in the early stages of any project. Prepare and research. Dwell on the problem for a while before rushing in with a premature solution. Einstein once said, "Give me six hours to chop down a tree and I will spend the first four sharpening the axe." Similarly, Michelangelo Buonarroti claimed that "if you knew how much work went into it, you wouldn't call it genius." We only see the very final step of the process, the vision manifest, and if the preparation has been done well, this step may appear rapidly and with seeming ease. In truth, though, those moments of genius have themselves probably been incubating for a long time.

Allow Yourself Time for Deep Thought and Reflection

Contemplation is a kind of action. Rest and become receptive. Let things roll around in your mind a little without guiding them in any direction. In your mind's eye, imagine the various stages of the project and mentally walk yourself through them before taking a single practical step. What are all the aspects of this project? Can you visualize potential problems? How might you prevent or mitigate them? How clear a picture of the end result can you imagine?

If you skip this step, or if your contemplation of the task is too shallow, then you will need to learn plenty of lessons the hard way. Your action will be characterized by lots of tweaks and corrections that could have been avoided had they taken place purely in the mind first. You might get far along in a project only to realize too late that the entire direction is wrong—a waste of time and energy.

After Contemplating, Proceed to Plan with Precision

The step between contemplation and action is planning. In your plan, you are gradually refining the process and making it more and more concrete. Leonardo recorded precise measurements in his notebooks, ensuring that every detail was meticulously considered. This step involves creating a detailed plan or strategy, breaking down the project into manageable tasks, and setting specific goals. The emphasis is on careful planning to ensure that execution is smooth and successful; however all this should only be attempted once the bigger picture, open-ended reflection, has run its course. There is no value in being very detailed and precise about an overall concept that has been poorly sketched out in the mind.

Rest Purposefully

The mind—even a genius mind—has its limitations. Just as our muscles can become fatigued, so, too, can our brains. Sleep and rest are so much more than just the empty spaces around "real work." Healthy rest is like the pauses between music notes or the white space on a written page—it's not *nothing*. In fact, it gives everything else structure and meaning. The interplay between silence and noise, black and white, and rest and work, is where something new can emerge. If we allow it, that is.

Whatever your goals and whatever area of study you're working in, try to learn to notice signals that you are getting tired and need time to replenish. If you're studying, do so in short bursts with frequent mini breaks where you stand up, stretch your legs, sip something, briefly switch tasks, or simply rest quietly while your brain catches up. Know your limits and aim for moderation. A well-timed nap or afternoon off can actually lead to more productivity in the long term than overworking and burning out later.

You may need to set serious boundaries with anyone or anything that threatens to encroach on your rest and reflection time—or the person you need to be firm with may be you! How you relax doesn't matter too much, but going out into nature, moving your body, sleeping, socializing, or engaging in a gentle and entirely unrelated hobby are all ways to stop and allow your creative juices to build up again. One surprising side effect of more deliberate and strategic rest periods is that you may find yourself less drawn to procrastination. This can happen when we ignore our fatigue signals and blast through, then misinterpret our own waning attention and energy as "laziness."

A Note on Procrastination

Was da Vinci a procrastinator? Are you?

Who knows. This term "procrastination" does not really have a rigorous, clear definition, which probably also explains why there are dozens of suggested solutions for it in popular media, many of them contradictory.

The tendency to put off work you believe you should be doing can come down to many things. It's up to you to understand exactly what you're doing (or not doing), and why, if you hope to be a little more focused and intentional. What works for one person may not work for another. What's more, what one person considers procrastination is merely harmless creative chaos and nothing to worry about.

To strike any meaningful balance between doing and not doing, you'll need to be observant and honest with yourself. Only you know what is at play in your own head and how your unique combination of skills and limits come together as you try to tackle your chosen area of learning. That said, there are a few questions to help you better understand your predicament if you find that putting things off is getting in the way.

Are you feeling genuinely inspired by your task? Not everything has to be painfilled and highly entertaining, but feeling bored by a task *might* be a sign that you have outgrown it or that it's not ambitious or meaningful enough. If your project fired you up initially but leaves you cold now, try to understand exactly where your interest went, and act accordingly. The goal may be too big or too small, or too vaguely defined. You may be fearful and avoidant because you're overwhelmed—in that case cut things down to more manageable chunks. You may have simply gotten mired in irrelevant details, and it's time instead to remind yourself of why your task really matters.

How do you feel after forcing yourself to do five minutes of the task? Sometimes, there's no deep psychoanalytic reason for your procrastination. Human beings can be lazy, and they definitely can prefer to do a task that is easier and more pleasurable instead of one that would take a little more effort. Feeling this way now and then is not a character flaw, but failing to challenge it can be. You will know that you're dealing with garden-variety laziness and inertia if you feel more able to continue once you've started and done a little.

The same is true if you feel accomplished and proud of yourself after you've completed what seemed like a daunting task at first. The solution for you will not be to reassess your goals or try to understand where your passion went. Your solution will be old-fashioned discipline and forcing yourself to act. Remember that sometimes, we build motivation and inspiration by acting. If we wait around until we feel moved to act, we may be waiting a long time.

Finally, are you actually procrastinating in the first place? Who says that human beings should have the ability to focus perfectly and consistently in neat, hour-long chunks? Who says that every project that's started needs to be completed? On the other hand, who says that feeling bored, stuck, or uninspired about your work is necessarily a sign that you should stop at once?

Deciding that you are a procrastinator is more of a cultural diagnosis than a personal one. It can speak to our expectations around what we feel we *should* be doing—and these obligations may or may not align with reality. We sometimes assume that we are procrastinating when what we really mean is "I don't want to do this" or "This task holds no meaning for me." Real life puts all of us in this position sooner or later, but our response should not be to question our motivation or work ethic. If you are consistently resentful of certain tasks, try to see if you can automate them, delegate them, or simply find a way to not do them. Have you put this unmovable burden on yourself?

Feeling that you procrastinate could be a sign that your life lacks pleasure, joy, and levity in other areas, or that you are simply demanding too much of yourself and you just need a break. It could be telling you that your job is simply not working anymore—all jobs contain some degree of tedium, but if the tedium outweighs the sense of purpose or meaning, then your "procrastination" is a rational response to the situation.

One of the smartest and most accomplished human beings was labeled lazy and scatterbrained. This should tell us something: Human beings are not machines, even the really capable ones, and it's not reasonable to expect that any of us are perfectly motivated, organized, disciplined, and committed one hundred percent of the time. Hard work is hard. Our problem may be that we are expecting it to be easier!

Art and Science

"Sciences provide an understanding of a universal experience. Arts are a universal understanding of a personal experience . . . they are both a part of us and a manifestation of the same thing . . . the arts and sciences are avatars of human creativity."

Mae Jemison

Was da Vinci more of an artist or more of a scientist? Was he an artist who dabbled in science or a scientist who dabbled in art?

Perhaps both, perhaps neither—what we do know is that da Vinci was among those who didn't talk of science and art as mutually exclusive categories. Einstein thought that there was a single source of both art and science—the mysterious—and that accomplished scientists were almost indistinguishable from accomplished artists. Science fiction author Isaac Asimov thought that science and art were not distinct at all, but rather different aspects of the same whole. Da Vinci himself was said to have advised, "Study the art of science and the science of art."

In his book *The Story of Art*, art historian and author E. H. Gombrich explains how da Vinci was not just a dabbler who deliberately explored lots of different fields to supplement his life as a painter. Rather, Gombrich argues that his approach was to bolster his painting and elevate and expand the role of the artist.

Today we call anyone with such diverse interests and talents a Renaissance man, but perhaps da Vinci only saw his varied quests as an expanded curriculum to fulfill his life's work: his art, i.e., the pursuit and glorification of the sublime.

"It is likely that Leonardo himself had no ambition to be considered a scientist. All this exploration of nature was to him first and foremost a means to gaining knowledge of the visible world, such as he would need for his art," explains Gombrich. If he wanted to depict with honor and honesty the fullness of the human form, well then, he'd better understand what the human form *was*—the muscles, the skeleton, the biochemistry, the mechanics. In other words, if an artist wished to best depict and reflect reality, he had to understand that reality.

Da Vinci may have also wanted to elevate the profession itself and ennoble the social standing of painting. "He thought that by placing it on scientific foundations, he could transform his beloved art of painting from a humble craft into an honored and gentlemanly pursuit," says Gombrich. "To us, this preoccupation with social rank of artists may be difficult to understand, but we have seen what importance it had for men of this period."

What Gombrich is trying to show is that our conception of painting as a noble pursuit deserving a place alongside the sciences was due in large part to da Vinci's work. Before da Vinci, classical liberal education included things like logic, grammar, rhetoric, and mathematics. Da Vinci's genius was to elevate art so that it could also be included in these esteemed ranks.

Bear in mind that it was only in the twentieth century, many decades after da Vinci lived and worked, that scholars began to divide themselves into different disciplines. After years of such fragmentation, thought leaders are now looking back to the old Renaissance heroes and wondering if their original, holistic approach was perhaps preferable.

Da Vinci made careful and meticulous observations about the speed of birds' wings, comparing the tiny difference between the upward and downward strokes and producing two-dimensional works of imagined birds with exact curvature in their wings so lifelike that they almost seem to take flight off the page. He was fascinated by the detail of the anatomy of blood vessels and how their form perfectly reflected their function so that his diagrams of the circulatory system looked more like beautiful astrological maps or gracefully branching trees. Because he understood the delicate musculature in the human face, he could imbue his portraits with subtle shading and color that made them feel almost more real than real. This is not art *or* science—it's the distilled essence of the enraptured intellect, a picture of human curiosity interfacing with the mystery and wonder of the universe it inhabits.

Though the title of this chapter references balance, perhaps da Vinci would instead call his work "integrative." After all, the world we find ourselves in is all one piece and intricately connected; why should our study of it not reflect this interconnection? John James Audubon, Ada Lovelace, Louis Pasteur, and Buckminster Fuller are other such integrative artists who achieved greatness due to their same disregard for arbitrary limits on human inquiry. What can we learn from them?

Becoming Artful
Whatever area you currently devote your intellectual efforts to, how can you elevate your practice in the same way that da Vinci elevated painting? In *Quartz* magazine Ben Shneiderman shares research findings where medical professionals perform better at their jobs when also receiving training in the visual arts. By learning to study in depth certain museum pieces, for example, dermatologists were better

able to describe and identify certain skin lesions during examinations.

In the same vein, training medical professionals in certain kinds of music theory improved their ability to detect subtle changes in their patient's heartbeats or understand the various sounds coming from their lungs or stomachs. Einstein himself claimed that music was at the foundation of his theory of the insights that later became his theory of general relativity. It's what da Vinci understood long ago—art and our ability to *understand* a phenomenon are deeply connected.

Robert Root-Bernstein is a sociologist who has long been interested in science and scientists, and when he studied Nobel Prize winners, he found that all of them were polymaths—and they were *more* proficient at art, music, poetry, literature, theater, sculpture, etc. than the average person, not less.

Training in art is training in refined perception. By observing nature with a fresh, curious, and respectful eye, we find prototypes for new inventions. In dreams we first encounter novel concepts. In the whispers of trees, we hear the beginnings of a symphony (like Bach did as he walked through the forests to reflect). From art we can generate science, but it goes the other way, too: The tools we use, including the language, symbols, and narratives we use to interact with reality, end up giving us renewed insights into it; from perceiving science we can generate new art.

To become more artful and integrated yourself, it may be necessary to continually think beyond the artificial categories of the modern intellectual landscape and return to a more fluid, more nuanced (and frankly more beautiful) mode of knowledge, like the one inhabited by da Vinci and his ilk. Here are some ideas for bringing some of this depth and richness into your own life:

Don't Shy Away from the "Hard Sciences"

Start by exploring various scientific disciplines—even the ones you feel a little intimidated by. It doesn't matter if you cannot see a way to directly apply these ideas to your own pursuits—the benefit is in the *way* you're learning to think, not necessarily the *content* of what you're thinking about. Whether it's biology, physics, astronomy, chemistry, or any field that piques your interest, challenge yourself to dig a little deeper. If you are an artist, explore the properties of light and the deeper fundamentals of color mixing. If you're an athlete, learn more about the detailed chemistry of ATP production. If you're a programmer, dig into the science of the actual hardware you're using and how it works.

Too many of us are content to let the "experts" do the heavy lifting while we use the tools and gadgets they design without much further thought. But by doing so, we miss out on huge chunks of understanding and lose the opportunity to enrich the grasp we have on our own subjects, even if they're a world apart from the sciences.

Observe and Deduce

Train yourself to observe the world with a keen eye. The eye of an artist is not all that different from the eye of a scientist. Both are trying in their own way to really *see what is*. Notice details in nature, human anatomy, and the built environment. Look more closely at the tools and materials in your environment without taking any of it for granted. Da Vinci's meticulous observations of the human body, for instance, greatly influenced his ability to represent it accurately in his art.

Connect scientific principles to artistic concepts. Understand how light, color, form, and structure align with scientific theories. Da Vinci's ability to merge his scientific insights with his art allowed him to create works that were not only aesthetically pleasing but scientifically informed. Art and science can mutually give feedback to one another. Let the eye of the poet help you perceive widely and with nuance; let the mind of the scientist observe and gather data. What you learn can then be interpreted again by the heart of the storyteller, who shapes the concrete details gathered by the hands of the architect or designer . . .

The Importance of Interdisciplinary Learning
Interdisciplinary thinking, exemplified by the likes of Leonardo da Vinci, holds profound advantages in our rapidly evolving world. It not only equips individuals to navigate technological shifts and societal changes but also broadens their knowledge base, fostering the creation of innovative insights.

Actively seek opportunities to develop skills that span multiple disciplines. Emulate Da Vinci's approach by combining seemingly unrelated skills to enhance your problem-solving abilities and creativity. Leverage online resources and educational platforms to create a personalized learning journey. Be intentional about exploring subjects beyond your immediate expertise. Set aside dedicated time to watch videos, read articles, or take courses that expand your knowledge horizontally, mirroring Da Vinci's broad interests.

Finally, don't underestimate the power of collaboration, both with those in your field and those far outside of it. An individual man can be a Renaissance man, but so much the better to construct a *Renaissance community* around yourself. In your professional and personal pursuits, actively seek to act as a bridge between disciplines, encouraging diverse perspectives and insights. Put people in contact who otherwise wouldn't have encountered one another. Have outlandish discussions or propose unexpected shared projects.

Liat Segal is a media artist interested in the fusion of art and technology, and Shimon Adaf is an author, writer, and poet. They explain how an interdisciplinary program at Tel Aviv University is changing the way that universities structure their students' learning journey. The program is open-ended and lets students create their own paths of learning and develop their mental flexibility by following their own interests and curiosity. Students in the program can pick up courses from across the institution, designing their own curriculum as they go, whether they choose mathematics, neuroscience, art, physics, poetry, or something else entirely. For example, Segal chose computer science, psychology, history, art courses, and biology—a combination you won't find in a conventional university!

Segal explained, "The program is supposed to be four years, but usually it takes much longer because when you get to the time you're supposed to choose what you're doing . . . you just realize that you didn't do it all."

Segal initially worked at Microsoft Innovation Lab but is now a full-time artist. She's seen firsthand how this cross-pollination between separate sectors leads to fresh waves of creativity and innovation. Working closely with one another, people from all backgrounds, talents, and interests all converse and offer one another different lenses through which to understand their own work, uncovering fresh perspectives. Segal now actively encourages entrepreneurs to look widely for inspiration and to challenge themselves to broaden and develop their education as thinkers and creators in a rapidly changing world.

In Frans Johanssen's book *The Medici Effect*, we learn of a powerful example of interdisciplinary innovation: Students at Brown University from the neuroscience, biology, and computer science departments teamed up to create a groundbreaking implant that allowed monkeys to move a computer cursor with their minds—a feat impossible to imagine had each department kept to itself.

Granted, not all of us are destined for scientific breakthroughs of this kind, but we can apply some of the thinking to our own projects. If you're interested in something, explore it, whether it "fits" or not! Remember that you don't have to be excellent at it, just try it out and see what happens. Connect with other generalists and get the conversation going. Experiment often and be willing to try out lots of different things. Almost always, the network's magic is not in the individual nodes, but in the connections between them.

Mirror Writing

"If art reflects life, it does so with special mirrors."

Bertolt Brecht

One of da Vinci's most fascinating and enigmatic habits was to write in his notebooks backward. His use of mirror writing has intrigued scholars and enthusiasts for centuries, and while his exact motivations remain uncertain, several theories offer insights into this unique aspect of his work.

One prominent theory suggests that mirror writing served as a method of ensuring the privacy and secrecy of his extensive notes and ideas. In the competitive intellectual environment of his time, using reverse writing could have functioned as a form of code or encryption, making it challenging for others to decipher his observations in fields like anatomy, engineering, and science.

Another theory ties Leonardo's left-handedness to his use of mirror writing. As a left-handed writer using ink and quill, writing in reverse may have been more practical, preventing smudging and ensuring a cleaner writing surface. Additionally, some scholars propose that mirror writing might have been a personal quirk or preference for Leonardo, reflecting his unconventional thinking and creative mindset—in other words, a stylistic choice. His notebooks, filled with sketches, scientific diagrams, and observations, often showcased his experimental approach to various subjects, and there's no reason to imagine that such a person wouldn't experiment with the aesthetics of his written expression, too.

Technical considerations are also part of the discussion, with suggestions that the nature of Leonardo's notebooks or the tools he used may have influenced his choice of mirror writing. Given his involvement in scientific studies that involved looking through mirrors, this technical aspect could have played a role in shaping his writing style. We might never fully understand the symbolic value of this idiosyncrasy and how it fit into da Vinci's main body of work. We are intrigued, however, and this may point to something important—the sheer whimsy of sometimes being, quite literally, a little backward.

Da Vinci was documented as a rather eccentric person and was not afraid to buck traditions of all kinds. He never married and little is known of his love life, but he was accused of sodomy in 1476, and most historians agree that he was almost certainly a homosexual. He was also a vegetarian (vanishingly rare in those days), a redhead (considered freakish in the fiftieth century), wore his hair and beard long when the fashion was for both to be short, and donned clothing in colors and styles considered unbecoming for his age.

So why did he write backward? Well, nobody can say for sure. The most probable but least glamorous answer is the same answer to the question "Why did he choose to wear bright-pink tights?" which is "Because he wanted to." Da Vinci was nothing if not an original; he took nothing for granted and questioned *every* convention. He was the sort of person to notice that writing was done left to right, with the right hand, and decided to investigate: Why do we do that? What happens when we do something else?

Perhaps da Vinci had some special affinity for the science and symbolism of mirrors. Or perhaps, just as with the woodpecker's tongue, there may be no mystery of the universe hidden in this line of inquiry ... but rather something to play with simply for curiosity's sake.

It's interesting to note that da Vinci was not the only one to practice this kind of writing, and that it was relatively common during that time period.

Should You Learn to Write Backward?
Granted, the act of writing something backward is not a groundbreaking discovery or likely to lead to any astounding insights, but there may be good reason to try it out for yourself.

Learning to write with your non-dominant hand is an interesting experience—your brain is suddenly asked to attempt the very familiar in a way that's totally new and unexpected. In a way, being a beginner again gives you fresh insight into the fundamental mechanics of what you're doing. You're like a child again, and suddenly far more aware of all those separate skills that you previously took for granted. You may not easily be able to say exactly how you write with your dominant hand, but if you do it with your non-dominant hand, you can far more easily identify what the separate steps are and exactly what it takes to get the pen to do what you want.

It's this additional awareness that may be behind the value of writing backward. A 2017 meta-analysis by GD Schott in the *Journal of Neurology, Neurosurgery, and Psychiatry* offered a few interesting observations about mirror writing. Schott noted that the phenomenon is almost always found in left-handed people, and people who use "leftward" languages, i.e., those written right to left (that explains Sultan Bayezid, then!).

There are more interesting facts, too:

- Mirror writing can be classified as deliberate, spontaneous, or acquired involuntarily.
- Mirror writing has been found to exist in both individuals of identical sets of twins and

has reappeared within the same three generations of a family.
- "Usually, the line of mirror writing flows from right to left, but sometimes—as in Chinese script—normal leftward hieroglyphs can be reversed, but not the rightward ordering of the vertically written lines," the author claims, "and mixtures of orientations of letters, words, and lines of writing may be seen."
- There have been reports of people who perform *upside down* mirror writing.
- Some individuals have been recorded to spontaneously acquire the ability after a brain lesion, stroke, or other injury.
- The ability to mirror write is occasionally paired with the ability to mirror read.

While research in this area is rather limited, there is reason to believe that the brain and the directionality of writing are closely connected. If the brain can be altered to produce reversed writing, then perhaps reversed writing is a way to alter the brain? In fact, Schott conjectures that da Vinci's ability to write backward was related to a stroke he sustained at some point in adulthood.

The Case of the "Mirror Man"
Research by Robert MacIntosh and his team focused on the case of Kasimir Bordihn, who is

right-handed when writing but had been practicing deliberately with his left hand in a mirror image for over fifty years at the time of the study. By studying his performance, the researchers concluded that Bordihn's left hand was executing a motor handwriting program that had already been developed by his right hand, almost as though the right hand becomes the teacher and the left the student.

The idea goes that over years of repetition and learning, the right hand is programmed with a series of special movements and sequences. When these are transferred across the body's midline to the other hand, they reflect, almost as though in a mirror. The same muscles are being activated in the same way, but reversed.

The researchers go on to suggest that, seeing as the right brain hemisphere controls the movements of the left hand and vice versa, mirror writing may strengthen the connections between the neurons, in the corpus callosum especially. If you are right-handed, for example, your left-brain hemisphere is the one to have developed the motor program for writing, and it needs to figure out a way to send this program to the left hand (which is controlled by the right hemisphere of the brain). This effort may result in increased "inter-hemisphere information transfer," which itself has been suggested as a marker for high intelligence.

In addition to cognitive benefits, mirror writing may impact memory positively. The unique and challenging nature of this task likely stimulates brain function, contributing to improved memory retention. Furthermore, the deliberate and focused nature of mirror writing may enhance overall concentration skills, demanding precision and attention to detail.

So, is it worth learning to mirror write? Possibly! If you're curious to try it out, it's simple to begin:

1. Grab a piece of paper and make two columns.
2. Write a passage from a favorite book in the right column.
3. Copy it in the left column but mirror the letters.
4. Repeat!
5. As you progress, strive for consistency and legibility in your mirrored text. Gradually increase the complexity of the passages you choose to mirror write.

If you complete a pair of pages a day, you'll soon notice—like the mirror man did—that your performance quickly improves. You may even detect that the handwriting made by the dominant hand improves, too. Though there is too little research to say just how much mirror writing you have to practice before you can notice any effects, this is perhaps part of the charm: By doing your own experiments and monitoring yourself, you can experience the outcome firsthand.

If mirror writing doesn't appeal, don't worry, the principle likely applies to other activities, too. Try to think of ordinary tasks you do every day that require ingrained motor patterns, then practice doing them in a reverse or upside-down way. Brush your teeth with a different hand, lead with your non-dominant leg when walking, or even just sit in a different position or posture than you ordinarily would. By slightly mixing up your ordinary patterns, you not only give yourself a chance to look with fresh eyes at what you're doing, but you also give your brain a mini workout by asking it to find balance within itself.

Summary:

- Leonardo da Vinci suffered from distractibility and procrastination, but this may have been part of his genius rather than something that undermined it. Creativity often does entail delays and proceeds in fits and starts. Varying energy, motivation, and clarity levels are normal.
- It's up to us to find a balance between doing and not doing. Before diving into a project, take the time to thoroughly study and research the subject matter before taking the first step. Allow yourself time for deep

thought and reflection, and only after you thoroughly understand the task, proceed with a detailed and meticulous plan.
- If you procrastinate, be honest about the causes and take appropriate action. Decide whether you need more discipline or more insight into your goals and deeper motivations/purpose. Realize, however, that some procrastination is par for the course.
- Rest purposefully and respect your own limitations, putting up boundaries where necessary so your body and mind can properly recharge.
- Rethink any mental divisions between art and science and seek an integrative approach that looks to the deeper root of both. Challenge yourself to inquire into ideas you think are outside your field, i.e., cultivate interdisciplinarity.
- Create your own *renaissance community* by collaborating with others in different areas and designing a broad, all-encompassing curriculum for your self-study.
- Dabble, if you like, with mirror writing to challenge your brain and throw fresh insight into old skills you currently take for granted, or else practice doing habitual things in slightly different ways.

Conclusion

"A beautiful body perishes, but a work of art dies not."

Leonardo da Vinci

It was 1519 when Leonardo da Vinci died, and the world felt his loss. Vasari spoke of his "outstanding physical beauty, infinite grace, great strength and generosity, regal spirit, and tremendous breadth of mind." Sculptor and goldsmith Benevenuto Cellini said, "There had never been another man born in the world who knew as much as Leonardo, not so much about painting, sculpture, and architecture, as that he was a very great philosopher."

Today, the Piazza della Scala in Milan is graced with a sculpture commemorating da Vinci's contributions to the world. The statue has four of his pupils at the corners of its base—Giovanni Antonio Boltraffio, Marco d'Oggiono, Cesare da Sesto, and Gian Giacomo Caprotti—and at the center top stands Leonardo in his characteristic robes, long hair, and Renaissance-era cap. The artist, now himself depicted as a work of art, looks down thoughtfully at something—perhaps his pupils, perhaps the world. Or perhaps his attention is turned inward, contemplating something subtle, mysterious, and as yet unseen by the outward eyes.

The inscription beneath it is a dedication:

"TO THE RENOVATOR
OF THE ARTS AND SCIENCES
BORN IN VINCI DI VALDARNO
IN THE MCCCCLII
DIED IN CLOUX NEAR AMBOISE
IN THE MDXIX
LONG AN ENVIED GUEST
IN MILAN, WHERE HE HAD
FRIENDS, DISCIPLES, GLORY
ON THE FOURTH DAY OF SEPTEMBER
OF MDCCCLXXII
THIS MONUMENT
WAS PLACED."

The monument earned its fair share of criticism both when it was erected in 1872 and afterward (can you imagine the pressure to produce something worthy?). But the truth is that Leonardo's legacy stood on its own long before it was formally cemented in sculpture. His esteem survived him, and his plentiful notebooks spoke for themselves, being written in that universal human language that is comprehensible to all who are powered by a deeper yearning: curiosity. But beyond that, da

Vinci's notes and paintings speak more eloquently than any biography or scholar could about the truth and beauty the painter was always, throughout his life, trying to gesture toward.

We see echoes of the great man's ideas and ideals all throughout our modern world, and modern art and science owe much to this one-of-a-kind illegitimate child born more than five hundred years ago now. As we end our own tribute to the great Leonardo di ser Piero da Vinci, we can remind ourselves of the attributes and virtues he possessed that gave his life the glory he is known for today. Of course, there is and can only be one da Vinci, but by the same token, there is only one of each of us—how can we use the lessons from his life to inspire and elevate our own?

Principle 1: Be curious, be curious, be curious!

"Learning never exhausts the mind."

If there was an engine at the heart of da Vinci's life, it was the insatiable lust to know more, to understand, to comprehend. Your first promptings of interest and fascination are precious—they are often the first step in a long journey of learning.

Regularly ask yourself what currently fires you up. What are you deeply curious, nosy, and intrigued by? What puzzles you?

Principle 2: Look to nature for guidance, wisdom, and inspiration

According to da Vinci, human intelligence will "never devise an invention more beautiful, more simple, or more direct than does nature." No matter what your endeavor is, nature is a good place to start. "Nature is the source of all true knowledge. She has her own logic, her own laws, she has no effect without cause nor invention without necessity."

Ask yourself how nature solves the problem you are currently experiencing, or what medium she might express the idea that you're trying to grasp yourself. Let her be your first mentor.

Principle 3: Be an original

Commit yourself to follow your own intuition and principles, many of which will only become clearer to you if you are able to be still in solitude and reflect without the pressures of convention. Be brave enough to follow a different path, if necessary.

"If you find from your own experience that something is a fact and it contradicts what some authority has written down, then you must abandon the authority and base your reasoning on your own findings."

Principle 4: Be courageous, experiment, and work hard

That said, you are the easiest person to fool, and your biggest challenge will not be to master nature or other people, but *yourself*. Be honest, ask questions, and be courageous enough to accept the answers you get, or else admit that you don't know. Commit first to never deceiving yourself, then take inspired and intelligent action to understand more about your world.

If you don't understand something, do an experiment, ask a question, or seek a teacher—anything to bring your inquiry into real life. "I have been impressed with the urgency of doing. Knowing is not enough; we must apply. Being willing is not enough; we must do."

Principle 5: Seek to elevate

Find beauty and transcendence where you can, or else create it. There is splendor and magic in science and mathematics, and there is law and reason in poetry and painting. Seek them both.

"Observe the light and consider its beauty," da Vinci advises. "Blink your eye and look at it. That which you see was not there at first, and that which was there is there no more." Your quest for truth can only be improved by expanding it to include this kind of awe, wonder... and a hint toward some divinity beyond. "Where the spirit does not work with the hand, there is no art."

Even in the smallest tasks you attempt, how can you elevate your work to its highest potential?

Principle 6: Be proactive

"It had long since come to my attention that people of accomplishment rarely sat back and let things happen to them. They went out and happened to things."

If you wait for permission before you act, or become too attached to the validation and approval of conventional authorities, you will never have a chance to do something unique, exceptional, or new. Da Vinci taught himself; he did not wait for someone to bestow the answers on him.

How can you take inspired action right now, instead of waiting for someone else to do it for you?

Principle 7: Keep striving for excellence and virtue

"Iron rusts from disuse; water loses its purity from stagnation... even so does inaction sap the vigor of the mind."

Never stop asking how you can be better. Look inward and make connections within your own mind and constantly cultivate and organize what powers you were gifted with so that you're always fulfilling your highest potential—whatever that may look like for you.

Principle 8: Make room for rest and reflection

Taking breaks and time for reflection is not about rewarding yourself for hard work or letting yourself off the hook. It's about gaining psychological distance, fresh perspective, and the chance to see what cannot be seen if you are too engrossed in a project.

"Every now and then go away, have a little relaxation, for when you come back to your work your judgment will be surer. Go some distance away because then the work appears smaller and more of it can be taken in at a glance and a lack of harmony and proportion is more readily seen."

Summary Guide

CHAPTER 1: FROM APPRENTICE TO MASTER

- Leonardo da Vinci was a Renaissance-era polymath, painter, inventor, scientist, artisan, draughtsman, philosopher, botanist, sculptor, and musician. By studying his life and philosophy, we can imbue our own lives with a little of his famous curiosity.
- The first step is to secure an appropriate mentor. Born to humble beginnings, da Vinci was self-taught and apprenticed himself at the age of fourteen to a master painter who tutored him. He was diligent and deferred to him in all things, understanding the importance of consistent practice and training.
- Follow the correct mentoring process, beginning with deep observation (passive mode), then skills acquisition (practice mode), and finally experimentation (active mode).
- A good mentor should be a genuine expert in their field, know how to get the most from their students, and not be threatened if the student surpasses them. They should be able to demonstrate open-mindedness to

- approaches other than their own and be able to point to past students who have excelled.
- Be mindful of your environment, which is also a kind of tutor, influencing the character and development of your thought. Seek a diverse and open environment where bustle, competition, cooperation, newness, and difference are the norm. Be welcoming to outsiders and outsider thought, embracing interdisciplinarity with others unlike yourself. Find ways to collaborate and connect.
- To be a Renaissance reader, develop a consistent habit of both reading and note-taking. Build daily routines based in a well-crafted learning environment, and actively engage with the text, continually comparing it against your goals and intentions. Read widely, diligently, and strategically ... and do it every single day.

CHAPTER 2: THE MIND OF THE POLYMATH

- The most fundamental trait of a lifelong learner like da Vinci is an attitude of insatiable curiosity. Shift your mindset toward a focus on unanswered questions. Be childlike and continually experiment with

different perspectives. Keep a running list of open questions to guide and inspire your learning.
- The right attitude is patient enough to practice learning as a lifelong pursuit, humble enough to engage with mistakes and the unknown, and practical enough to use real-world experience to inform one's mental models.
- An elastic mind is healthy in the same way that a body is healthy: It can change, and it is strong, flexible, and responsive to its environment. Where the mind is flexible and able to grow and adjust, innovation, exploration, creativity, and novelty are possible.
- Elastic thinking requires dynamism, adaptability, courage, and a love for the unconventional—although it always anchors in the known.
- Da Vinci's principle of "sensazione" reminds us that learning should never be purely intellectual, but multisensory. Renaissance men were fully rounded and highly developed in sense perception. You can develop this capacity in yourself by slowing down, practicing synesthesia, and engrossing yourself in nature with senses fully switched on.

CHAPTER 3: A MAP OF THE INTELLECT

- Leonardo Da Vinci is often referred to as a "T-shaped" individual due to his wide range of talents and expertise paired with impressive depth in some areas; today he'd be called a versatilist. To become more of a T-shaped person yourself, first assess your current skills and base knowledge to determine where skill and knowledge are lacking. Honestly appraise your current skill level and identify which areas need improvement, maintenance, addition, or work to increase depth.
- Then, even if you are already in a structured training program, devise your own curriculum and be disciplined in following your own learning goals according to what you discover in the above exercise—don't simply default to other people's values and principles. Set consistent habits to work on your goal daily and have a means to monitor your progress.
- Keep a balance of hard and soft skills. Know what your priorities are, but don't be afraid to dabble now and then just out of curiosity.
- One of the polymath's greatest skills is the ability to connect the unconnected. You can use da Vinci's attribute technique to

systematically uncover fresh ideas and combinations. Break the problems down into a series of parameters and then brainstorm as many variations/attributes as possible for each that you can. Run through the table of possibilities without preconceptions or judgment to uncover new possibilities.
- In a similar way, get comfortable with the language of metaphor, which not only helps us to grasp more complex or abstract ideas, but it also helps us generate those ideas.

CHAPTER 4: GET ORGANIZED

- Getting organized is about bringing "a series of small things together" so that new insight, connection, and understanding can be obtained. Proper note-taking helps you clarify, extend, and deepen your understanding of your work, and acts like a "second brain."
- Your best note-taking system will be one you devise yourself, but experiment with end-of-page summaries, special notations, questions and comments in the margins, mind maps, and links to other material. Make it fluid and flexible. Use the two-page da Vinci technique to enter into a "dialogue" with your notes that you continually prune

and update. Don't forget to bring a small notebook wherever you go!
- A to-do list can be re-imagined as a to-learn list—not based on dull obligation but on interest and curiosity. Mundane chores cannot be avoided, but try to *prioritize* your spontaneous interest and capture fresh ideas when they emerge, taking detailed notes and returning to them later. This may require a deep mindset shift about the divide between work and play and between "should" and "want to." Try to cherish and cultivate your inborn wonder, rather than squashing it in the name of productivity and efficiency.
- Archimedes' eureka moment can teach us a lot about rest, downtime, and obliquely solving problems rather than structured, forceful slogging. We often find insight in the least expected place, when our minds are free to play, explore, and connect randomly.
- Deliberately embrace rest, breaks, unstructured time, and open-ended doodling. Change perspectives and find fresh solutions by regularly stepping back from your work.

CHAPTER 5: STRIKING A BALANCE

- Leonardo da Vinci suffered from distractibility and procrastination, but this may have been part of his genius rather than something that undermined it. Creativity often does entail delays and proceeds in fits and starts. Varying energy, motivation, and clarity levels are normal.
- It's up to us to find a balance between doing and not doing. Before diving into a project, take the time to thoroughly study and research the subject matter before taking the first step. Allow yourself time for deep thought and reflection, and only after you thoroughly understand the task, proceed with a detailed and meticulous plan.
- If you procrastinate, be honest about the causes and take appropriate action. Decide whether you need more discipline or more insight into your goals and deeper motivations/purpose. Realize, however, that some procrastination is par for the course.
- Rest purposefully and respect your own limitations, putting up boundaries where necessary so your body and mind can properly recharge.
- Rethink any mental divisions between art and science and seek an integrative approach that looks to the deeper root of both. Challenge yourself to inquire into ideas

you think are outside your field, i.e., cultivate interdisciplinarity.
- Create your own *renaissance community* by collaborating with others in different areas and designing a broad, all-encompassing curriculum for your self-study.
- Dabble, if you like, with mirror writing to challenge your brain and throw fresh insight into old skills you currently take for granted, or else practice doing habitual things in slightly different ways.

www.ingramcontent.com/pod-product-compliance
Lightning Source LLC
Chambersburg PA
CBHW061747070526
44585CB00025B/2822